**OPPOSING
VIEWPOINTS®
SERIES**

Celebrity Culture

Other Books of Related Interest:

Opposing Viewpoints Series

American Values

Children and the Entertainment Industry

The Culture of Beauty

At Issue Series

Beauty Pageants

Can Celebrities Change the World?

Reality TV

Current Controversies Series

Media Ethics

Rap Music and Culture

"Congress shall make no law . . . abridging the freedom of speech, or of the press."

First Amendment to the U.S. Constitution

The basic foundation of our democracy is the First Amendment guarantee of freedom of expression. The Opposing Viewpoints Series is dedicated to the concept of this basic freedom and the idea that it is more important to practice it than to enshrine it.

OPPOSING VIEWPOINTS® SERIES

Celebrity Culture

Roman Espejo, Book Editor

GREENHAVEN PRESS
A part of Gale, Cengage Learning

GALE
CENGAGE Learning™

Detroit • New York • San Francisco • New Haven, Conn • Waterville, Maine • London

Christine Nasso, *Publisher*
Elizabeth Des Chenes, *Managing Editor*

© 2011 Greenhaven Press, a part of Gale, Cengage Learning

Gale and Greenhaven Press are registered trademarks used herein under license.

For more information, contact:
Greenhaven Press
27500 Drake Rd.
Farmington Hills, MI 48331-3535
Or you can visit our Internet site at gale.cengage.com

For product information and technology assistance, contact us at

Gale Customer Support, 1-800-877-4253
For permission to use material from this text or product, submit all requests online at www.cengage.com/permissions

Further permissions questions can be emailed to permissionrequest@cengage.com

Articles in Greenhaven Press anthologies are often edited for length to meet page requirements. In addition, original titles of these works are changed to clearly present the main thesis and to explicitly indicate the author's opinion. Every effort is made to ensure that Greenhaven Press accurately reflects the original intent of the authors. Every effort has been made to trace the owners of copyrighted material.

Cover image copyright Andrejs Pidjass, 2010. Used under license from Shutterstock.com.

LIBRARY OF CONGRESS CATALOGING-IN-PUBLICATION DATA

Celebrity culture / Roman Espejo, book editor.
 p. cm. -- (Opposing viewpoints)
 Includes bibliographical references and index.
 ISBN 978-0-7377-5213-7 (hbk.) -- ISBN 978-0-7377-5214-4 (pbk.)
 1. Fame--Social aspects--Juvenile literature. 2. Celebrities--Juvenile literature.
 3. Popular culture--Juvenile literature. I. Espejo, Roman, 1977-
 BJ1470.5.C46 2010
 306.4--dc22   2010032979

Printed in the United States of America
1 2 3 4 5 6 7 14 13 12 11 10

Contents

Why Consider Opposing Viewpoints?

> *"The only way in which a human being can make some approach to knowing the whole of a subject is by hearing what can be said about it by persons of every variety of opinion and studying all modes in which it can be looked at by every character of mind. No wise man ever acquired his wisdom in any mode but this."*
>
> John Stuart Mill

In our media-intensive culture it is not difficult to find differing opinions. Thousands of newspapers and magazines and dozens of radio and television talk shows resound with differing points of view. The difficulty lies in deciding which opinion to agree with and which "experts" seem the most credible. The more inundated we become with differing opinions and claims, the more essential it is to hone critical reading and thinking skills to evaluate these ideas. Opposing Viewpoints books address this problem directly by presenting stimulating debates that can be used to enhance and teach these skills. The varied opinions contained in each book examine many different aspects of a single issue. While examining these conveniently edited opposing views, readers can develop critical thinking skills such as the ability to compare and contrast authors' credibility, facts, argumentation styles, use of persuasive techniques, and other stylistic tools. In short, the Opposing Viewpoints Series is an ideal way to attain the higher-level thinking and reading skills so essential in a culture of diverse and contradictory opinions.

In addition to providing a tool for critical thinking, Opposing Viewpoints books challenge readers to question their own strongly held opinions and assumptions. Most people form their opinions on the basis of upbringing, peer pressure, and personal, cultural, or professional bias. By reading carefully balanced opposing views, readers must directly confront new ideas as well as the opinions of those with whom they disagree. This is not to simplistically argue that everyone who reads opposing views will—or should—change his or her opinion. Instead, the series enhances readers' understanding of their own views by encouraging confrontation with opposing ideas. Careful examination of others' views can lead to the readers' understanding of the logical inconsistencies in their own opinions, perspective on why they hold an opinion, and the consideration of the possibility that their opinion requires further evaluation.

Evaluating Other Opinions

To ensure that this type of examination occurs, Opposing Viewpoints books present all types of opinions. Prominent spokespeople on different sides of each issue as well as well-known professionals from many disciplines challenge the reader. An additional goal of the series is to provide a forum for other, less known, or even unpopular viewpoints. The opinion of an ordinary person who has had to make the decision to cut off life support from a terminally ill relative, for example, may be just as valuable and provide just as much insight as a medical ethicist's professional opinion. The editors have two additional purposes in including these less known views. One, the editors encourage readers to respect others' opinions—even when not enhanced by professional credibility. It is only by reading or listening to and objectively evaluating others' ideas that one can determine whether they are worthy of consideration. Two, the inclusion of such viewpoints encourages the important critical thinking skill of objectively evaluating an author's credentials and bias. This evaluation will illuminate an author's reasons for taking a particular stance on an issue and will aid in readers' evaluation of the author's ideas.

It is our hope that these books will give readers a deeper understanding of the issues debated and an appreciation of the complexity of even seemingly simple issues when good and honest people disagree. This awareness is particularly important in a democratic society such as ours in which people enter into public debate to determine the common good. Those with whom one disagrees should not be regarded as enemies but rather as people whose views deserve careful examination and may shed light on one's own.

Thomas Jefferson once said that "difference of opinion leads to inquiry, and inquiry to truth." Jefferson, a broadly educated man, argued that "if a nation expects to be ignorant and free ... it expects what never was and never will be." As individuals and as a nation, it is imperative that we consider the opinions of others and examine them with skill and discernment. The Opposing Viewpoints Series is intended to help readers achieve this goal.

David L. Bender and Bruno Leone,
Founders

Introduction

> *"There's a societal structure that we've built, in part thanks to television, that says this is the thing you want, desire, and aim for."[1]*
>
> —*Matthew Smith,*
> *chairman,*
> *Department of Communication,*
> *Wittenberg University*

On October 15, 2009, a runaway homemade balloon in Fort Collins, Colorado, ignited a media storm. Designed by storm chaser and amateur scientist Richard Heene, the silver saucer-like contraption allegedly carried away his six-year-old son, Falcon, around 11:00 a.m. The Heenes first called the Federal Aviation Administration, then local station KUSA-TV and 9-1-1. Coverage of the event was instantly ubiquitous; live footage of the floating balloon was broadcast around the world. "Balloon Boy," the nickname for Falcon, became the top search on Google, and parodies went viral on social networking sites.

In efforts to rescue Falcon, the Colorado National Guard dispatched helicopters to track the balloon, and flights were temporarily grounded at the Denver International Airport. At 1:30 p.m., the balloon landed northeast of Denver, traveling sixty miles before deflating. The boy was not found inside, fueling speculation that he had fallen out during flight. But three hours later, reports surfaced that Falcon had hid in the rafters of the family's garage, afraid that his parents would be angry with him. Reporters and cameras swarmed the Heenes' home as the family celebrated their son's safety.

1. "Is Child Exploitation Legal in 'Kid Nation'?" *Los Angeles Times*, August 17, 2007. http://articles.latimes.com.

However, their story began to unravel just as swiftly. On *Larry King Live*, Falcon blurted out that they "did this for the show," and the boy became nauseated during interviews on *Good Morning America* and *TODAY* when pressed about his statement. Furthermore, the Heenes' backstory came to light. Richard and his spouse, Mayumi, were former actors who appeared on the reality TV program *Wife Swap*. Richard had also unsuccessfully pitched a science show to TLC months before, and prospects for another TV program had crumbled. Authorities eventually discovered that the whole ordeal was staged for publicity. Richard and Mayumi were sentenced to jail, fined $36,000, and prohibited from profiting from the story.

In the wake of the "Balloon Boy" hoax, critics assailed the reality television trend, which exploded during the last decade in the United States, transforming ordinary people into celebrities overnight. "[O]nly in the reality TV era has unstable behavior become a valid career choice,"[2] claimed James Poniewozik, a television critic for *Time*. "None of us can really know the dynamic of the Heenes or how eager Richard's wife and children were to serve his scientainment ambitions," he added. "But that doesn't make turning their lives into TV a better idea or make exploiting them in a publicity scheme any less odious." Some experts expressed particular concern for children, like Falcon and his brothers, Ryo and Bradford, who appear on such programming. "The child stars who are not on reality TV, they understand that what they're doing is a story, it's fantasy,"[3] clinical psychologist Nadine Kaslow explained. "For these reality kids, this is about their lives—they're not just characters. It's about them."

Yet, other observers proposed that the Heenes deserved some sympathy. Television writer and producer Norman Lear accused the media of "creating a climate that mistakes enter-

2. *Time*, November 2, 2009. www.time.com.
3. *Good Morning America*, October 20, 2009. http://abcnews.go.com./GMA.

tainment for news,"[4] which convinced Richard and Mayumi "into believing they are—even if what they dream up to qualify is a hoax—entitled to their fifteen minutes." Likewise, Frank Rich, a *New York Times* op-ed columnist, held networks responsible for fanning the fire of the "Balloon Boy" saga: "Richard Heene is the inevitable product of this reigning culture, where 'news,' 'reality' television, and reality itself are hopelessly scrambled, and the warp-speed imperatives of cable-Internet competition allow no time for fact-checking."[5] And Rich viewed Richard Heene's scheme as a desperate bid for financial security, not fame, in a recession. "There's also some poignancy in his determination to grab what he and many others see as among the last accessible scraps of the American dream," he wrote.

With series such as *Survivor, American Idol,* and *America's Next Top Model* continuing season after season, reality television lures thousands of Americans like the Heenes, who seek fame and fortune—or validation and stability—to nationwide auditions and, if they're lucky, scrutiny on the screen. *Opposing Viewpoints: Celebrity Culture* investigates this phenomenon and the culture of fame in the following chapters: "Is Celebrity Culture a Problem?" "How Does Celebrity Culture Affect Young People?" "Does Celebrity Activism Benefit Society?" and "What Is the Future of Celebrity Culture?" The authors—social commentators, scholars, and journalists—attempt to place star power in contexts both public and personal.

---

4. *Huffington Post*, October 21, 2009. www.huffingtonpost.com.
5. *New York Times*, October 24, 2009. www.nytimes.com.

OPPOSING
VIEWPOINTS®
SERIES

CHAPTER 1

Is Celebrity Culture a Problem?

Chapter Preface

The sudden death of Anna Nicole Smith eclipsed not only her dramatic, often controversial life as a sex symbol, reality TV star, and heiress, it gripped the nation in a "feeding frenzy" of media coverage in 2007. From the day she died, (February 8) to her burial in the Bahamas (March 2), only two other stories received more attention—the war in Iraq and the upcoming U.S. presidential election—according to the Pew Research Center's Project for Excellence in Journalism (PEJ). In the first few days, PEJ claims that 55 percent of cable news airtime, 25 percent of online news, and 17 percent of newspaper's front-page news was dedicated to Smith. "Overall, across all media sectors studied, the celebrity better known for her measurements than accomplishments accounted for 30 percent of the coverage in those first two days,"[1] PEJ states. Still, PEJ insists that cable news networks left the impression that Smith's death was a "wall-to-wall event from which there was no escape," devoting almost a quarter of its broadcasting to the story for more than three weeks.

In line with PEJ's skeptical view of Smith's notoriety, the immense media attention that her death generated sparked criticism. When the story broke, NBC anchor Brian Williams said on a newscast, "This may say a lot about our current culture of celebrity and media these days, when all the major cable news networks switched over to nonstop live coverage this afternoon when word arrived that Anna Nicole Smith had died."[2] In addition, Paula Zahn, then a newscaster on CNN, contended that the fascination with Smith reflected "America's fixation on celebrity, on tragedy, on sex, money, tabloid head-

---

1. PEJ Special Index Report, April 4, 2007. www.journalism.org.
2. PEJ Special Index Report, April 4, 2007. www.journalism.org.

lines, and death."[3] The day after, blogger Leslie McClinton wrote, "Besides being from Texas, posing for *Playboy*, and marrying a rich old man, what had Anna done? Exactly."[4]

Other commentators, however, defended the headlines about the high school dropout and former waitress, born Vicki Lynn Hogan. Jack Shafer, a writer for *Slate*, asserted that her legal battle for a $500 million fortune, the onslaught of paternity claims for her newborn daughter, and the mysterious circumstances of both her son's and her own death provided a complex narrative that was stranger than fiction. "To stay on top of the Smith story once it got going, you really had to pay attention,"[5] he maintained. "Far from being useless pop entertainment, cable's coverage taught viewers reams about civil procedure, pharmacology, and police work." And Smith's obituary in the *Sunday Times* stated, "The fact that the circumstances of her brief marriage, in her mid-twenties, to Texas oil baron J. Howard Marshall II, sixty-three years her senior, were ever argued in the U.S. Supreme Court is testimony enough to Smith's astonishing determination."[6] In the following chapter, the authors deliberate on the consequences of society's captivation with celebrities.

3. PEJ Special Index Report, April 4, 2007. www.journalism.org.
4. Blogcritics.org, February 9, 2007. http://blogcritics.org.
5. *Slate*, April 4, 2007. www.slate.com.
6. February 10, 2007. www.timesonline.co.uk.

| *"Celebrity worship has banished the real
  from public discourse."*

Celebrity Culture Is Harmful

Chris Hedges

Chris Hedges is a senior fellow at the Nation Institute and author of Empire of Illusion: The End of Literacy and the Triumph of Spectacle. *In the following viewpoint, Hedges contends that celebrity culture drowns out public discourse and encourages materialism and self-absorption. He states that gossip and chatter dominate what really matters in the nation—the wars in the Middle East, politics, the economy, and the environment. Moreover, the glossy lifestyles of the rich and famous, Hedges insists, are held up as aspirations for disenfranchised Americans who can no longer sustain themselves on the lies manufactured by the media.*

As you read, consider the following questions:

1. How does the author characterize the public in contrast to celebrities?

2. What does celebrity culture view as desirable, as stated by Hedges?

3. According to Hedges, how does celebrity culture create desperation and loss of touch with reality?

Will Tiger Woods finally talk to the police? Who will replace Oprah? (Not that Oprah can *ever* be replaced, of course.) And will Michaele and Tareq Salahi, the couple who crashed President Barack Obama's first state dinner, command the hundreds of thousands of dollars they want for an exclusive television interview? Can Levi Johnston, father of former Alaska Gov. Sarah Palin's grandson, get his wish to be a contestant on *Dancing with the Stars*?

The chatter that passes for news, the gossip that is peddled by the windbags on the airwaves, the noise that drowns out rational discourse, and the timidity and cowardice of what is left of the newspaper industry reflect our flight into collective insanity. We stand on the cusp of one of the most seismic and disturbing dislocations in human history, one that is radically reconfiguring our economy as it is the environment, and our obsessions revolve around the trivial and the absurd.

What really matters in our lives—the wars in Iraq and Afghanistan, the steady deterioration of the dollar, the mounting foreclosures, the climbing unemployment, the melting of the polar ice caps and the awful reality that once the billions in stimulus money run out next year we will be bereft and broke—doesn't fit into the cheerful happy talk that we mainline into our brains. We are enraptured by the revels of a dying civilization. Once reality shatters the airy edifice, we will scream and yell like petulant children to be rescued, saved and restored to comfort and complacency. There will be no shortage of demagogues, including buffoons like Sarah Palin, who will oblige. We will either wake up to face our stark new limitations, to retreat from imperial projects and discover a new simplicity, as well as a new humility, or we will stumble blindly toward catastrophe and neofeudalism.

Nothing Else in Life Counts

Celebrity worship has banished the real from public discourse. And the adulation of celebrity is pervasive. The frenzy around political messiahs, or the devotion of millions of viewers to Oprah, is all part of the yearning to see ourselves in those we worship. We seek to be like them. We seek to make them like us. If Jesus and [the best-selling book by Rick Warren] *The Purpose Driven Life* won't make us a celebrity, then [self-help author and speaker] Tony Robbins or positive psychologists or reality television will. We are waiting for our cue to walk on-stage and be admired and envied, to become known and celebrated. Nothing else in life counts.

We yearn to stand before the camera, to be noticed and admired. We build pages on social networking sites devoted to presenting our image to the world. We seek to control how others think of us. We define our worth solely by our visibility. We live in a world where not to be seen, in some sense, is to not exist. We pay lifestyle advisers to help us look and feel like celebrities, to build around us the set for the movie of our own life. [Television host and magazine publisher] Martha Stewart constructed her financial empire, when she wasn't engaged in insider trading, telling women how to create a set design for the perfect home. The realities within the home, the actual family relationships, are never addressed. Appearances make everything whole. Plastic surgeons, fitness gurus, diet doctors, therapists, life coaches, interior designers and fashion consultants all, in essence, promise to make us happy, to make us celebrities. And happiness comes, we are assured, with how we look, with the acquisition of wealth and power, or at least the appearance of it. Glossy magazines like *Town & Country* cater to the absurd pretensions of the very rich to be celebrities. They are photographed in expensive designer clothing inside the lavishly decorated set pieces that are their homes. The route to happiness is bound up in how skillfully we present ourselves to the world. We not only have to conform to the dictates of this manufactured vision, but we also have to project an unrelenting optimism and happiness. Hedonism and wealth are openly worshiped on Wall Street as well as on shows such as *The Hills, Gossip Girl, Sex and the City, My Super Sweet 16* and *The Real Housewives of* (whatever bourgeois burg happens to be in vogue).

The American oligarchy—1 percent of whom control more wealth than the bottom 90 percent combined—are the characters we most envy and watch on television. They live and play in multimillion-dollar mansions. They marry models or professional athletes. They are chauffeured in stretch limos. They rush from fashion shows to movie premieres to fabulous resorts. They have surgically enhanced, perfect bodies and are draped in designer clothes that cost more than some people make in a year. This glittering life is held before us like a beacon. This life, we are told, is the most desirable, the most gratifying. And this is the life we want. Greed is good, we believe, because one day through our acquisitions we will become the elite. So let the rest of the bastards suffer.

The working class, comprising tens of millions of struggling Americans, are locked out of television's gated community. They are mocked, even as they are tantalized, by the lives of excess they watch on the screen in their living rooms. Almost none of us will ever attain these lives of wealth and power. Yet we are told that if we want it badly enough, if we believe sufficiently in ourselves, we too can have everything. We are left, when we cannot adopt these impossible lifestyles as our own, with feelings of inferiority and worthlessness. We have failed where others have succeeded.

False Promises

We consume these countless lies daily. We believe the false promises that if we spend more money, if we buy this brand or that product, if we vote for this candidate, we will be re-

"Important News . . . Britney is having twins," cartoon by Terry Wise. www.Cartoon Stock.com.

spected, envied, powerful, loved and protected. The flamboyant lives of celebrities and the outrageous characters on television, movies, professional wrestling and sensational talk shows are peddled to us, promising to fill up the emptiness in our own lives. Celebrity culture encourages everyone to think of themselves as potential celebrities, as possessing unique if unacknowledged gifts. Faith in ourselves, in a world of make-believe, is more important than reality. Reality, in fact, is dismissed and shunned as an impediment to success, a form of negativity. The New Age mysticism and pop psychology of television personalities and evangelical pastors, along with the array of self-help best sellers penned by motivational speakers, psychiatrists and business tycoons, peddle this fantasy. Reality is condemned in these popular belief systems as the work of Satan, as defeatist, as negativity or as inhibiting our inner essence and power. Those who question, those who doubt, those who are critical, those who are able to confront reality, along with those who grasp the hollowness and danger of celebrity culture, are condemned for their pessimism or intellectualism.

The illusionists who shape our culture, and who profit from our incredulity, hold up the gilded cult of *Us*. Popular expressions of religious belief, personal empowerment, corporatism, political participation and self-definition argue that all of us are special, entitled and unique. All of us, by tapping into our inner reserves of personal will and undiscovered talent, by visualizing what we want, can achieve, and deserve to achieve, happiness, fame and success. This relentless message cuts across ideological lines. This mantra has seeped into every aspect of our lives. We are all entitled to everything. And because of this self-absorption, and deep self-delusion, we have become a country of child-like adults who speak and think in the inane gibberish of popular culture.

Celebrities who come from humble backgrounds are held up as proof that anyone can be adored by the world. These celebrities, like saints, are examples that the impossible is always possible. Our fantasies of belonging, of fame, of success and of fulfillment are projected onto celebrities. These fantasies are stoked by the legions of those who amplify the culture of illusion, who persuade us that the shadows are real. The juxtaposition of the impossible illusions inspired by celebrity culture and our "insignificant" individual achievements, however, is leading to an explosive frustration, anger, insecurity and invalidation. It is fostering a self-perpetuating cycle that drives the frustrated, alienated individual with even greater desperation and hunger away from reality, back toward the empty promises of those who seduce us, who tell us what we want to hear. The worse things get, the more we beg for fantasy. We ingest these lies until our faith and our money run out. And when we fall into despair we medicate ourselves, as if the happiness we have failed to find in the hollow game is our deficiency. And, of course, we are told it is.

A New Dark Age

I spent two years traveling the country to write a book on the Christian Right called *American Fascists: The Christian Right and the War on America.* I visited former manufacturing towns, where for many the end of the world is no longer an abstraction. Many have lost hope. Fear and instability have plunged the working class into profound personal and economic despair, and, not surprisingly, into the arms of demagogues and charlatans of the radical Christian Right who offer a belief in magic, miracles and the fiction of a utopian Christian nation. Unless we rapidly re-enfranchise these dispossessed workers, insert them back into the economy, unless we give them hope, these demagogues will rise up to take power. Time is running out. The poor can dine out only so long on illusions. Once they grasp that they have been betrayed, once they match the bleak reality of their future with the fantasies they are fed, once their homes are foreclosed and they realize that the jobs they lost are never coming back, they will react with a fury and vengeance that will snuff out the remains of our anemic democracy and usher in a new dark age.

> "Celebrity, far from being a shallow ar-
> tifice, often addresses the fundamental
> differences between the real and the
> false, the meaningful and the meaning-
> less."

Celebrity Culture Is Beneficial

Neal Gabler

*In the following viewpoint, Neal Gabler asserts that celebrities'
lives provide enriching human narratives. People learn about
love, family, and the pitfalls of fame and wealth through entertainment news and tabloids. The advantages of celebrity culture
over movies, novels, plays, and television, Gabler further proposes, is that it takes place in reality and does not have closure,
which makes it more satisfying for audiences. In fact, the author
states that stories and news about celebrities unify the politically
and socially fractured American public. Gabler is a senior fellow
at the Norman Lear Center at the University of Southern California and author of* Life the Movie: How Entertainment Con-
quered Reality.

As you read, consider the following questions:

1. How does the author define a celebrity?

2. According to Gabler, what do the best celebrity narratives achieve?

3. How does Gabler describe Brad Pitt and Angelina Jolie?

By now you've probably heard of or seen Jaimee Grubbs explaining that her relationship was emotional, not just physical, or Mindy Lawton describing an attraction to red underwear, or Jamie Jungers revealing who underwrote her liposuction. They are everywhere on tabloid television shows, personal-interest magazines, and supermarket scandal sheets. And just who are Jaimee Grubbs, Mindy Lawton, and Jamie Jungers? They are three of Tiger Woods's alleged mistresses— women with no ostensible talent or accomplishment to justify the attention save to expose their private lives for our titillation. In short, they are the epitome of modern celebrity.

That isn't a compliment. "Celebrity" has become a tarnished word, for which we may largely credit the late Daniel Boorstin, the eminent historian who defined it in *The Image*, his 1961 survey of what he saw as the devolution of America. "The celebrity," Boorstin proclaimed, "is a person who is known for his well-knownness." Boorstin was writing at a time of great cultural flux, with the rise of the mass media and an effulgence of what he considered trash, and he placed celebrity within the larger context of an America whose citizens were increasingly enthralled by imitations of reality rather than by reality itself—by the pretense of substance without the actual substance. He coined the term "pseudo-event" to describe counterfeit happenings like press conferences, photo ops, and movie premieres that existed only to advertise themselves. He called celebrities human pseudo-events: hollow façades illuminated by publicity. So it has been ever since.

But there is a less antiquated and reproachful perspective on celebrity—one that may help explain why Michael Jackson, Britney Spears, Paris Hilton, and now the new and revised Tiger Woods seem so embedded in the national consciousness.

In this view, celebrity isn't an anointment by the media of unworthy subjects, even though it may seem so when you think of minor celebs such as [reality TV stars] Spencer Pratt and Heidi Montag, or [the former fiancé of Bristol Palin, Sarah Palin's daughter] Levi Johnston, or the [White House's] gatecrashing Salahis [referring to Michaele and Tareq Salahi, the couple who crashed President Barack Obama's first state dinner]. It is actually a new art form that competes with—and often supersedes—more traditional entertainments like movies, books, plays, and TV shows (and the occasional golf tournament), and that performs, in its own roundabout way, many of the functions those old media performed in their heyday: among them, distracting us, sensitizing us to the human condition, and creating a fund of common experience around which we can form a national community. I would even argue that celebrity is the great new art form of the 21st century.

To be honest, I didn't escape the temptation to trivialize celebrity myself when I wrote my own analysis 10 years ago in my book *Life the Movie*. I called celebrities not human pseudo-events but "human entertainments"—not people who existed to be publicized but people whose lives seemed to exist to provide us with ongoing amusement. By this analysis, celebrities weren't just awarded publicity for no good reason; they received publicity because they provided narratives for us. Michael Jackson's life was a long, fascinating soap opera that included not only his success but also his tiffs with his family, his erratic behavior, his plastic surgeries, his bizarre marriages, his masked children, his brushes with the law, his alleged drug use, and finally his mysterious death. Ditto the life of Britney or Oprah or Brad [Pitt] and Angelina [Jolie] or anyone, even [reality show stars] Jon and Kate Gosselin, whose personal activities provide us with entertainment.

But what I failed to appreciate then is that human entertainment is not simply a carnival personified. In fact, celebrity really isn't a person. Celebrity is more like a vast, multicharacter show, albeit with a star, only it is performed in the medium of life rather than on screens or on the stage and then retailed in other media. No media, no celebrity. Technically speaking, then, celebrities don't have narratives. Celebrity is narrative, even though we understandably conflate the protagonist of the narrative with the narrative itself and use the terms interchangeably. That is why one can be famous, as Queen Elizabeth is, without necessarily being a celebrity, as Princess Di [Princess Diana] was. One has name recognition, the other a narrative.

To see the truth of this, you can apply a very simple test. A so-called celebrity is a celebrity only so long as he or she is living out an interesting narrative, or at least one the media find interesting. Indeed, even non-entertainers or people not ordinarily in the public eye can be grazed by the celebrity spotlight if they live a compelling enough narrative, which is how a Joey Buttafuoco [who made headlines in 1992 when his underage mistress shot his wife] or a Nadya Suleman [single mother of octuplets] or even one of Tiger's mistresses receives celebrity treatment. Typically, the size of the celebrity is in direct proportion to the novelty and excitement of the narrative—to wit, Michael Jackson and Britney Spears. When an individual loses his or her narrative or the narrative becomes attenuated, the celebrity vanishes—the equivalent of a movie or a novel that bores you. He or she is relegated to "Where are they now?"

This still doesn't account for the popularity of celebrity in a world where there are so many narratives to choose from, so many different forms of entertainment. Here Boorstin may have an answer. One of his complaints in *The Image* was that the democratization of culture had marginalized older art forms that could no longer satisfy a larger public as fully as the new ones did. He cited the movies as having driven the novel into psychology because the movies had preempted action and did it better than novels could, whereas the movies were less capable of plumbing inner depths. That left novels with a new franchise but with a significantly smaller readership.

Something similar seems to have happened in the competition between celebrity and other, older art forms. So many of our movies, novels, plays, and television programs have subsisted on providing us with verisimilitude so that we feel what we are watching or reading is real; with identification so that we either believe the people whom we are watching or about whom we are reading are like us or like our fantasies; with stakes so that we imagine what happens to them really matters; and with suspense so that we are riveted because we need to know what is going to happen next. These are the staples of entertainment.

Given these ingredients, celebrity has tremendous advantages over its more traditional, and fictional, competitors. For one thing, celebrity doesn't have to create the pretense of reality; it is real. The stories are enacted in life, which is why, aside from the inherent drama of hookups and breakups, sex has featured so prominently in celebrity narratives. (So has violence.) There is an almost voyeuristic frisson in knowing that this isn't simulated as it is in the movies. Nor does celebrity have to labor at creating identification; celebrity protagonists are almost, by definition, culturally preselected on the basis that we identify with them (Everyman) or enjoy a vicarious attachment through them (Superman). And because there are real consequences to the events in the narratives—people actually divorce or fall off the wagon or die—something is always at stake. We don't have to suspend our disbelief.

Finally, celebrity possesses suspense that older forms can only manufacture. That's because traditional forms have closure—an ending when you turn the last page or when the lights go up or when the credits roll. But celebrity narratives have no final chapter. We don't know whether Brad and Angelina will stay together or have more children or cheat on one another or decide to join a monastery. We don't know what new revelations will arise about Tiger Woods. We don't even know the truth about Michael Jackson's death yet. We are always awaiting the next installment: the next romance, drug binge, arrest, incarceration, mental breakdown, pregnancy, accident—you name it.

And all this provides yet another, extra-aesthetic satisfaction that conventional entertainments can seldom supply. Long before celebrity reached its apotheosis, the great gossip columnist and radio broadcaster Walter Winchell, who purveyed the malfeasance and transgressions of the rich, the famous, and the powerful to tens of millions of Americans, understood that celebrity was a basis for an ongoing, daily national conversation that also served as therapy to a wounded country, albeit with a savage subtext of revenge. Reaching his own peak in the Depression '30s at a time of anxiety and fractiousness, Winchell managed to unify his readers and listeners around his narratives, not only distracting them from calamity but also giving them a rallying point of common reference that was every bit as powerful as the national symbolism that FDR [President Franklin Delano Roosevelt] promoted. Winchell turned us into a nation of yentas [busybodies or gossips].

This function is especially potent today in another time of uncertainty and division, when Americans are not only disunited over politics and values, but also share fewer and fewer common experiences. In the past, television, movies, music, even books were sources of national cohesion. Dramatically lower ratings for broadcast television, reduced film attendance, and plummeting CD sales have all loosened the national bonds. We have become a nation of niches. Celebrity is one of the few things that still crosses all lines. As disparate and stratified as Americans are, practically all of them seem to share an intense engagement, or at the very least an acquaintance, with the sagas of Jon and Kate or Brad and Angelina or

Jennifer [Aniston] and whomever, which is oddly comforting. These are America's modern denominators, and in some ways Jon and Kate are our Fred [Astaire] and Ginger [Rogers, entertainers from the 1930s]—not, obviously, talentwise, but in the way they provide escape and give us something we can all talk about.

Still, it denigrates our favorite movies, television shows, novels, and plays to think of them as merely providing us with mindless escapism or subjects for conversation. Like all good art, the best of them resonate with us because they provide us with life lessons or because they capture the cultural moment or because they give us a glimpse of transcendence or because they stimulate the imagination. The best of celebrity has that capacity too, and just as the most complex films, novels, and plays have layers of meaning and even profound truths, so do the best and longest-lasting celebrity narratives, like Jackson's or Marilyn Monroe's or the Kennedy family's. These themes can convert a celebrity narrative from fact to metaphor, from entertainment to art, from gossip to an epic novel.

Reading *People* or *Us* or [celebrity gossip blogger and television personality] Perez Hilton, we learn variously about the joys of new love and the hurts of the old, the satisfactions of parenthood, the wages of sin, the punishment for hubris, the drawbacks to fame as well as its blessings, the risk of losing yourself and the exhilaration of finding yourself, and, perhaps above all, the things that really matter in life and the things that don't, which means that celebrity, far from being a shallow artifice, often addresses the fundamental differences between the real and the false, the meaningful and the meaningless. These are the concerns to which we have always turned to art to explain. Even the Speidi [referring to reality TV stars Spencer Pratt and Heidi Montag] story has a postmodernist subtext about identity, reinvention, the lust for fame, and envy that tells us something significant about ourselves and our society if we have the tenacity to dissect it.

In effect, then, we have invented celebrity and latched onto it because celebrity does a better job of giving us what traditional art and entertainments once gave us before they became too enervated to surprise us, or we became too jaded to be surprised. By the same token, in a symbiotic turn, many protagonists of celebrity narratives have become sophisticated enough to realize that they could recast their narratives as a way of sustaining their own celebrity, turning their life into their work. One will never know how much of Michael Jackson's eccentricity was a way to keep his narrative (and his celebrity) going, though we can be fairly certain that his decision to return to performing was intended as another chapter in his story: Michael's Comeback! We don't know how much of Lindsay Lohan's behavior is a way to keep herself in the public eye when she has no movies to do so. And we don't know how much Madonna's abrupt career changes and public romances are her way of manipulating celebrity to her benefit. We do know the effect.

On the other hand, even people who seem to resist creating narratives that might attract tabloid attention, a grande dame like Meryl Streep or a Hollywood nice guy like Tom Hanks, are sucked into the celebrity narrative vortex not because their lives are especially salacious or sensational but because their enormous talent and their success are themselves stories about which people want to hear or read. The *Los Angeles Times* recently ran a front-page article on Streep for no other reason than that she is America's most celebrated actress—a small narrative fillip. The story of developing talent and succeeding with it is a standard celebrity tale—though, as Tiger Woods discovered, the bland success story can rapidly transmogrify into an entirely different sort of narrative when more prurient elements present themselves. In any case, celebrity casts a wide net—not just pathology but also "feel-good."

To which one could add this irony: [author] J.D. Salinger is a celebrity largely by creating a narrative in which he abjures not only celebrity but also society.

The upshot is that celebrity narratives today are so effective, so ubiquitous, and so vigorous that they overwhelm virtually every other entertainment and art form, even the ones in which entertainers originally made their names. Brad Pitt and Angelina Jolie, to use just one example, are far better known for their life together than for the films they make, and there is no doubt that more people read about them or watch their exploits on *Entertainment Tonight* and *Access Hollywood* than attend their films. One might even say that their lives are such a big entertainment that their films are now a product of their celebrity rather than a source for it, to the point where their celebrity narratives can actually obscure their work, making it harder for an audience to accept them as the characters they play.

Yet it is not only that celebrity has triumphed over more traditional forms; it has, like cultural kudzu, subordinated the media generally. Since celebrity is a narrative in the medium of life, it requires magazines, newspapers, television shows, and perhaps most especially the Internet to promote it—a service these media happily perform and from which they get great residual benefits. As a result, the media are filled with celebrity narratives, constantly hawking them so that celebrity is to America today what the movies and television were to earlier generations, only more so. It is almost as if celebrity hangs ever-present in the ether where no previous entertainment has ever existed. We practically breathe it.

And so today we are gripped by Tiger Woods's story, and when his disappears, as it eventually will, another narrative will arrive and then another and then another, ad infinitum. That is how celebrity works—as a kind of endless daisy chain that amuses us, unifies us, and even occasionally educates us.

> "Overall, it is possible to see how the circus of celebrity culture is becoming an arena in which real issues are being played out before the public gaze."

Celebrity Culture Should Be Criticized

Mick Hume

In the following viewpoint, Mick Hume alleges that celebrities must be scrutinized because their objectionable actions mirror the state of the world. For example, the involvement of Madonna, Angelina Jolie, and other Hollywood figures in African countries spotlights imperialist Western attitudes and policies, Hume says. He adds that salacious media coverage of celebrity divorce and relationship scandals demonstrates how the line between the public and private is being redrawn. The famous, unlike politicians, however, are not held accountable for the damage they cause, Hume concludes. Hume is editor of spiked, *an independent Web magazine based in London, England.*

As you read, consider the following questions:

1. What is "caring colonialism," in Hume's opinion?

Mick Hume, "When Celebrities Rule the Earth," *Spiked*, October 24, 2006. Reproduced by permission.

2. What do celebrity tragedies and deaths reflect about the public, in Hume's view?

3. Why is the separation of the private and public important to the author?

You might have noticed that in recent months [in 2006] *spiked* writers—and none more so than me—have expended considerable effort writing about celebrity culture. If we are not lambasting [chef] Jamie Oliver's healthy eating crusade, we are criticising the involvement in Africa of everybody from [singer and political activist] Bob Geldof to Brangelina [referring to actors Brad Pitt and Angelina Jolie] and Madonna. No sooner have we finished questioning public reactions to [TV host] Steve Irwin's death or [British TV presenter] Richard Hammond's accident, than we launch into the muck-throwing circus surrounding the McCartneys' divorce [referring to the divorce of singer Paul McCartney and his wife, Heather Mills].

So why would *spiked* writers be so interested in the flotsam and jetsam of the celebrity world? Actually, some of us are not that interested—at least not in the antics of the individuals concerned. But we are concerned about the broader impact of celebrity culture in helping to reshape public life.

Often Symbolic

The main criticism people direct at the media obsession with celebrities is that it clogs up the news with trivia. But it matters more than that today. As serious public and political life has withered, so celebrity culture has expanded to fill the gap, often with the encouragement of political leaders desperate for some celebrity cover. What happens in the phoney world of celebrity is often symbolic of developments in the real world that affect us all—and rarely for the better.

Take the fuss over Madonna. Since I criticised her high-profile attempt to adopt a Malawian toddler, irate pundits from around the world have asked how anybody could want to make that boy live in poverty in Africa. In fact the argument is not really about Madonna and her new trophy baby. What she is doing embodies the new 'caring colonialism' underpinning Western attitudes towards Africa. It is based on the assumption that we know what is best for them, and the West must save Africans from themselves (see the father's latest claim that nobody told him they were taking his son away for good).

This popular attitude effectively reduces the whole of Africa to a helpless orphan that must be carried on our backs, just as Madonna carried her chosen 'son' for the cameras in a native sling. And it rides roughshod over any notion of African self-determination—consider Madonna's attempt to rewrite Malawi's law against foreign adoptions, or the way that Angelina Jolie and Brad Pitt effectively took control of Namibia's immigration laws to protect them from the press earlier this year. The implications become clearer still when Hollywood figures like George Clooney start fronting campaigns for more international military intervention in Darfur.

Shallow celebrities and their PR [public relations] machines did not invent these patronising attitudes of course. They take their lead from today's political campaigns on African poverty, led by high-powered statesmen such as UK [United Kingdom] chancellor Gordon Brown. But such grey-suited initiatives excite little interest. It tends to be only when an earnest celebrity such as Geldof or a glamorous one such as Madonna becomes involved that the issue of Western attitudes towards Africa and the developing world come under the media spotlight. The celebrity red carpet smoothes the way for further interference, often pushing the boundaries of what can be done further and faster than anything in formal politics.

It is a similar story on other issues where politicians who lack genuine public authority or appeal of their own seek to hide behind TV personalities. In this, at least, Jamie Oliver truly is a role model. His campaign on school meals has made far more impact than the government's endless droning on about healthy eating. In so doing, however, it has intensified the unhealthy and unjustified preoccupation with what we eat and the scaremongering about children's health. Whatever his intentions, Oliver has been acting as a mouthpiece for New Labour's parent-bashing message—but unlike politicians, the self-righteous celebrity is considered beyond serious criticism. Thus when Tory front-bencher Boris Johnson made some mild criticisms of the TV cook's campaign, he was not only forced to withdraw the remarks but the Conservative conference immediately passed an emergency motion hailing Oliver as a 'national hero'. When any celebrity is placed on a political pedestal like that, those who put him there need to be brought back to Earth.

A Wider Importance

Other developments in celebrity culture today help to throw the spotlight on wider problems in society. The bizarre global reaction to the death of Crocodile hunter Steve Irwin, for example, and the way that the world seemed to gather at the hospital bed of BBC *Top Gear*'s Richard Hammond, both highlighted the way that celebrity death or tragedy now seems to be one of the few things around which people feel able to 'come together', if only on the Internet. *spiked* writers have been upbraided for challenging these reactions. But (unlike certain others) we were not criticising the individuals at the centre of the dramas. Our arguments concern the way that such spasms of mawkish celebrity worship expose the lack of anything more meaningful or durable around which people can focus collective emotions and feel any sense of community today.

Similarly, we have no wish to get involved in the divorce scandals now surrounding Sir Paul McCartney and Heather

Mills. But the way that the gory details of their relationship have been splashed across the media has assumed a wider importance. This celebrity divorce case is now on the frontline of the battle to redraw the line between what should be private and public in society. It is rewriting the law on what can be made public, and accelerating the slide into exhibitionism and surveillance in our tell-it-all culture. The importance of this goes way beyond salacious gossip for those of us who want to defend the idea of both a proper public sphere where we can debate serious questions, and a private sphere where people can live and think as they see fit.

Overall, it is possible to see how the circus of celebrity culture is becoming an arena in which real issues are being played out before the public gaze. In a society without genuine heroes and leaders it can respect, many are drawn to celebrities and personalities who command affection, and can now use it to influence everything from African aid policy to the contents of a child's lunch box. The appeal of their campaigns is often based on the perception that they are not like politicians. Indeed they are not. For a start, nobody elected them to speak for us. And they are not accountable for the impact they make.

On *spiked*, we try hard not to be too po-faced or sanctimonious about celebrity. If people want to have fun following their favourite personalities, fair enough. But it is another matter when our trashy celebrity culture starts to colonise the public sphere and shape debate on political and social issues. So criticising the creeping advance of the celebrity empire seems likely to be a continuing theme on *spiked*—at least until the Next Big Thing comes along.

| "We can . . . look to our ancestors to explain celebrity worship."

Celebrity Culture Has Evolved over Time

Jeanna Bryner

Jeanna Bryner is managing editor of LiveScience, a science, technology, and health Web site. In the following viewpoint, Bryner proposes that the celebrity phenomenon is the product of human evolution and that it is psychologically rooted. She asserts that humans are innately social; they crave interaction and pay attention to the prestigious, successful, and beautiful. Interest in famous people varies from casual interest to celebrity stalking, and the practice is traced back to ancient civilizations and non-human primates, Bryner adds. Celebrity culture in modern society is on the rise, she states, because younger generations are more narcissistic and technology closes the distance between stars and their fans.

As you read, consider the following questions:

1. According to Bryner, what factors come into play for an individual's interest in celebrities?

Jeanna Bryner, "As Elvis Turns 75, Celebrity Worship Alive and Well," LiveScience, January 7, 2010. Reproduced by permission.

2. As described in the viewpoint, how is celebrity culture linked to human ancestors?

3. As stated by James Houran, why is obsession with celebrities similar to addiction?

If Elvis *were alive*, he'd be 75 on Friday [January 8, 2010]. While his musical style and gyrations may have been unique, Elvis Presley's stardom and swooning fans can be explained by simple psychology, trends in technology and pop culture, and a look at our ancestors, all of which reveals why celebrity worship is on the rise.

"The Elvis phenomenon is only a case study of a wider psychological phenomenon," said James Houran, a clinical psychologist and president of 20/20 Skills, a human resources company.

For obvious reasons—success, loads of money, looks—many people look up to celebrities, even after they've passed away. But other factors come into play, including:

- Personality type.

- Religion (the highly devout are less likely to worship stars).

- Psychological state (lonely individuals can take comfort in having a fantasy relationship with a star).

We can also look to our ancestors to explain celebrity worship. Humans are social beings who crave interaction with others, and we pay closest attention to the prestigious.

"We'll find those social relationships even when they're imaginary or illusory," said Adam Galinsky, professor at the Kellogg School of Management at Northwestern University. "Social hunger is really like ordinary hunger. It constantly needs to be satisfied but its satiation is short-lived."

That sector of the population most obsessed with celebrities, to varying degrees, is growing as a result of technology that lets us follow the George Clooneys of the world in nearly real time along with a rise in our society's narcissism, psychologists say.

Translation: Elvis impersonators and the like are here to stay.

Celebrity Stalkers

The degree of star-struckness goes from the healthy dose of flipping through *People* magazine to overboard and what scientists would categorize as a psychosis.

"There are people who really follow this stuff and find a celeb they really dig; they have Google alerts for them and they treat them like a friend or relative," said Cooper Lawrence, an expert on celebrity culture and fame. "Then there's a small percentage who [are] celebrity obsessed, where they really feel the celebrity is really talking to them," said Lawrence, who is the author of *The Cult of Celebrity*.

Elvis impersonators, she said, likely straddle these two levels.

The growing phenomenon of celebrity worship is affecting today's kids, too. Research reported in 2006 suggested celebrities dominated the interests of 7- to 11-year-olds even more so than toys and other products marketed to them. The researchers partly attributed the phenomenon to "our celebrity-obsessed society."

Celebrity Ancestors

Putting the rich and powerful on pedestals is nothing new.

"Every culture has its royalty of some sort and since we don't have any legitimate monarchy somebody has to serve that function," said Stuart Fischoff, emeritus professor of media psychology at California State University, Los Angeles, adding that we can look up to and even down on (when they slip up) these royal figures.

Fischoff also noted the Greeks and Romans had their own celebrities—Olympian gods.

"Cultural, anthropological and historical studies show us that human societies have always had a need to 'worship' things—and sure enough this was often special people in society—the best hunters, athletes, the most beautiful, the smartest, the most spiritual," Houran said.

As far back as our non-human ancestors, scientists have found evidence of focusing on the prestigious. That way, they would know how to gain rewards or avoid punishment, Galinsky said. He noted a study in which non-human primates gazed more at alpha males than others.

Why We Dig Celebs

The growing obsession with celebrities that are arguably not as worthy as, say, a great hunter-gatherer, is the result of various factors. For one, stars are right in front of our faces, being splashed across screens and in every form of media, according to Houran. Many of us like what we see and want to emulate that.

"Celebrities appear successful and are typically beautiful—qualities that naturally attract others because people tend to copy those who seem to have what we want," Houran told LiveScience.

Also "people quickly form illusory 'relationships' with celebrities since we learn much about them personally and feel we can relate to them in ways that maybe we cannot with our real friends and family," Houran said.

Some fans develop what they consider a real relationship with their celeb of choice. "They have a sense that, 'I am connected with that person, they know me and I know them,'" Fischoff said. "But the reality is it's a one-way street—they don't know who you are, unless you become a stalker."

A study published in a 2008 issue of the journal *Personal Relationships* showed that these one-sided relationships with celebrities could help low self-esteem individuals look at themselves more positively.

And indeed, social doors do open. "Some people make their lives have meaning because of their relationship with that celebrity. They develop a social network with other people who like that celebrity."

For the extreme fans, getting the scoop on their favorite famous person gives them a high.

"And finally for many people celebrity worship acts similar to addiction," Houran said. "Just like an addict developing a psychological or physical tolerance to a chemical substance, celebrity worshippers appear to need to endorse increasingly more intense or extreme attitudes and act out increasingly more intense or extreme behaviors in order to continue to feel connected to their favorite celebrity . . . or get a 'high' from celebrities."

Extreme Worship

Some people take celebrity watching more seriously, according to research.

For instance, religion matters. "The less religious you are the more likely you will worship celebrities," Lawrence said. "You'll be able to replace Jesus with George Clooney on some level. That's an extreme." The more religious person would kind of see this obsession as "worshiping false gods," she added.

"Certain people are more likely than others to succumb to the more extreme forms of celebrity worship," Houran said. Younger individuals are a high-risk group, he said, since there's a strong market for such celebrity idols and teens are vulnerable as they are just forming their personal identities.

Houran said others likely to do more than swoon at celebrity sightings would include: people who feel disconnected

Holding to Their Side of the Bargain

Even though we love to hear about the lavish rewards of fame—remember *Lifestyles of the Rich and Famous?*—we're quick to judge when stars behave too outrageously or live too extravagantly. We suspect some stars are enjoying society's highest rewards without really deserving them, says . . . anthropologist Robin Dunbar, so we monitor their behavior. "We need to keep an eye on the great-and-the-good because they create a sense of community for us, but also because we need to make sure that they are holding to their side of the bargain."

Carlin Flora,
"Seeing by Starlight: Celebrity Obsession,"
Psychology Today, *July 1, 2004.*

from society or have experienced a disruption in their identities, such as the recently divorced; depressed individuals; those with poor body image.

And the neurotics. "People who are tense, irritable, moody, antisocial, egotistical and impulsive tend to latch onto celebrities more easily than people low in these traits," Houran said.

On the Rise

Scientists say they have reasons to believe celebrity obsession is on the rise.

"People high in narcissism tend to embrace celebrity even more," Lawrence said. "A narcissist believes they are entitled to a certain way of treatment and a certain lifestyle, and who emulates that lifestyle more than a celebrity?" The present rise in celebrity culture, "where everybody is a celebrity, is directly correlated to the rise in narcissism," she said.

Why so many narcissists? Lawrence points to research suggesting some progressive parenting over the last decade or so could be partly to blame.

"Baby boomers and Gen-X parents are so afraid of ruining the self-esteem of their children. Everybody gets a trophy and my daughter is special; everybody has to be treated the same way," Lawrence said. "It's causing more narcissism because it's telling a kid you don't have to do anything to be successful, you just have to be wonderful fabulous you. They're great just for being born."

Then there's technology that's giving us record access to the rich and famous.

"While there has always been celebrity worship, technology has taken it to a heightened level," Houran said.

From entertainment news on TV to celebrity Web sites and social media, we are really getting to know these people.

"It does this by promoting in people the illusion that we can actually know and develop a relationship with celebrities. In essence, people seem to confuse having a lot of information about a celebrity with genuine intimacy," Houran said. "Now, more than ever before, technology allows fans to 'get closer' to their favorite celebrities. That is, the distance between fans and celebrities is getting smaller and smaller."

These huge windows into personal lives that are now so common arguably began with Elvis.

"Elvis really was one of the first to cross over into that type of celebrity," Lawrence said. "He was a singer and actor. He opened up his life to people, and people really felt like they knew him."

And while Elvis and [musician] John Mayer fans might have similar reasons for their obsessions, today's fans have higher expectations of celebs, Lawrence said. We expect all the intimate details of Mayer's love life, but as for Elvis: "They just wanted him to sing and be cute," she said.

| "*Perfect images of perfect celebrities are everywhere. It's enough to make anyone feel insecure or envious.*"

Celebrity Culture Promotes Unrealistic Body Images

Julie Mehta

In the following viewpoint, Julie Mehta contends that the flawless pictures and ads of celebrities can harm body image and self-esteem. Mehta states that these images can influence impressionable youths to view their bodies as not thin or fit enough. However, she counters that even stars themselves are retouched in photographs and do not live up to the standard of perfection reinforced by the media and advertising. Mehta advises that youths work on their self-esteem and eat and live healthfully to look and feel their best. Mehta is a writer in New York City.

As you read, consider the following questions:

1. As described by Mehta, what is the "digital diet"?

2. What is the result of media pressure and body image on boys, according to the author?

Julie Mehta, "Pretty Unreal: Ever Wish You Could Look as Hot as Celebrities Do? Well, They Don't Look as Good as You Think," *Current Health 2, a Weekly Reader Publication*, January 2005, p. 15(4). Copyright © 2005 Weekly Reader Corp. Reproduced by permission.

3. In Shari Graydon's view, how do others perceive our imperfections?

A sultry blonde stares back from a magazine ad, her mini-skirt revealing long, slender legs. An underwear model looms large on a billboard, flaunting his six-pack abs. A rock star sprawls across a CD cover, a belly button ring decorating her toned stomach.

And then there's you. You pass a mirror and glance at your image. What do you see? Maybe there's a zit on your forehead. Maybe the jeans that fit great last week now feel snug. You've heard it before: Nobody's perfect.

What's a person to think? Perfect images of perfect celebrities are everywhere. It's enough to make anyone feel insecure or envious. "The media sets up impossible comparisons. Whether you're watching sitcoms or music videos or looking through magazines, the images you're seeing are airbrushed and enhanced," said Shari Graydon, author of *In Your Face: The Culture of Beauty and You*. "And research shows that the more time kids spend with image-based media, the worse they feel about themselves."

Falling Short

Seeing all those artificially perfected images can hurt your body image— the way you see and feel about your body and the way you think others see you. From cartoon characters to movie stars, you have probably been exposed to messages about what is considered attractive as far back as you can remember. Those messages can seriously mess with your body image.

"I think the media has a big impact," 16-year-old Erika, of Scottsdale, Ariz., told *Current Health*. "It sets the standard—says thin is in. If the media wasn't saying skinny is appropriate, people wouldn't feel like they need to be so thin." According to Graydon, wanting to be thinner is a huge issue for many girls, while boys feel increasing pressure to be more buff. Boys look at singers such as Usher and realize they'll never have those abs—or the screaming female fans that go with them. In extreme cases, girls develop eating disorders and boys turn to steroids in an effort to achieve an ideal that isn't real.

"It's All Fake"

Celebrities and models are in the business of looking good, and they get a lot of help. Many follow special diets, and others have personal trainers who work with them for several hours a day. Just because they look fit doesn't mean they're healthy, though. Extreme diets can cause health problems, and compulsive workouts can lead to injury.

Despite models' best efforts, many still don't look "good enough" for the industry. "One hundred percent of fashion photos are retouched," said Brad Adams, a New York City photographer whose retouching service works with advertising agencies. "Usually the eyes and teeth are whitened, makeup and skin problems corrected, and hair cleaned up. Models are already thin, but I've done jobs where even skinny models are made to look skinnier."

Movie stars also receive the "digital diet" treatment, says a woman at another New York retouching service. "Even celebrity snapshots like those in *People*—the paparazzi shots—are retouched." She explains that Photoshop, a widely used software program, can digitally narrow hips or add to cleavage and make almost any change look realistic. "It's all fake," she added. "Nobody really has skin like that. All human beings have pores and get zits, and once they get rid of those, they have wrinkles."

Pursuit of Perfection

Why is everything touched up these days? "Magazines are supported by ads, and ads are about selling you a product," said author Jessica Weiner, who travels the country speaking to middle school and high school students about body image. "If you feel good about yourself, how many products will you buy? So [advertisers] have to make you feel like you need what they're selling by using unrealistic images." On a more basic level, the woman from the New York retouching company points out, "people like flawless and perfect images."

What, exactly, is perfection? "Different cultures and times define beauty differently," said Graydon. "In North America, large breasts are popular. But in Brazil, [women] get plastic surgery to have smaller breasts and bigger butts. And in Uganda and Peru, heavier women are seen as beautiful." Even in this country, ideals of beauty have shifted widely from generation to generation, from the voluptuous Marilyn Monroe in the 1950s to the waif-thin Kate Moss in the 1990s.

Ripple Effect

Perhaps you don't care what the media say you should look like. Still, you may be indirectly influenced by it through friends and family. "A lot of girls that I know always complain about their bodies," said Ashley, 14, of Wallingford, Conn. "It drives me crazy when they compare themselves to other people that they see in school or on TV."

Family members can also be culprits. If they constantly diet or pump up, you may follow their example—especially if they are concerned about your weight. "A lot of parents have gone through being teased and don't want their kids to go through that," said Kimber Bishop-Yanke, who runs self-esteem camps for girls in Detroit. "I see parents who are concerned their kids are getting fat, but it's normal to eat more and gain weight during puberty. It's just part of growing up."

Mirror, Mirror on the Wall

Of course, no one said growing up is easy. "I'm not fat, but I'm not skinny either," said 13-year-old Jordan, a seventh

Celebrity Worship and Body Image

Findings suggest that the type of interaction the individual has with the media is important in determining whether there is an effect on body image. Correlational research suggests three possible causal links between Intense-personal celebrity worship and poor body image. The first is that female adolescents who have Intense-personal feelings toward a celebrity with an attractive body shape develop a poor body image. The second is that those individuals who have a poor body image may develop an obsession with a media celebrity who they perceive as having a good body shape. The third, and perhaps most likely, is that the two processes are part of a cycle and that Intense-personal celebrity worship of a celebrity with a perceived good body shape leads to a poor body image, and that poor body image creates a deep interest in certain celebrities because of their body shape.

John Maltby, David C. Giles,
Louise Barber, and Lynn E. McCutcheon,
"Intense-Personal Celebrity Worship and Body Image:
Evidence of a Link Among Female Adolescents,"
British Journal of Health Psychology, *February 2005.*

grader from Baton Rouge, La. "I think I have big thighs, and when I wear shorts they stick out. A lot of kids tease me, but I try not to care so much."

Girls seem particularly prone to body-image issues. "When I was younger, it was harder because I wanted to fit in so much," admitted Natalie, 17, of Humphrey, Neb. Erika from Scottsdale added, "I'm in cheer, and most of my friends want to lose weight." She says she has dieted before and goes to the gym several times a week. Meanwhile, her classmate, Aliraza,

15, says he has never really worried about his looks. "I'm pretty sure girls have a lot more pressure when it comes to appearance."

Tim, a 14-year-old from New York City, agrees there is less pressure on boys than girls but says, "There is still some pressure—to be more buff." Experts, such as Roberto Olivardia, are starting to pay more attention to the effects of media pressure on boys. Olivardia, an instructor at Harvard University, co-wrote the book *The Adonis Complex: The Secret Crisis of Male Body Obsession*, which details a disorder among men that the authors call "bigorexia." Considered the reverse of anorexia, bigorexia occurs when a guy sees himself as puny no matter how muscular he is. Symptoms may include excessive time spent working out, constant grooming and mirror checking, and anabolic steroid use.

Bigorexia is one type of body dysmorphic disorder (BDD), a medical condition that equally affects males and females. BDD is an ongoing obsession with some small or imaginary problem with one's body. About one of every 50 people suffers from the condition.

Being True to You

Ultimately, body image has a lot more to do with your mind than your body. Self-esteem plays a huge role in body image, so the better you feel about yourself, the more likely it is you'll like what you see in the mirror. Whether you're slim or curvy, lanky or big, the keys to looking your best are eating right, exercising regularly, and feeling good inside.

"You're not your nose or butt or hair on a good or bad day," said Graydon. As a practical matter, "most people are way too distracted by their own imperfections to focus on yours," she added. What it all comes down to is that your body is your home for life. Given enough time, you may look back and laugh at the way you once fixated on your body's "flaws."

Natalie couldn't agree more. "As you get older, you get to be more comfortable with who you are, and you learn to be happy with yourself." Why not start by loving your body—and yourself—now?

> *"One can appreciate the assumption that by seeing our chubby 'role models' as often as we do on TVs and other platforms, it fuels the perception that obesity is 'normal.'"*

Celebrities and Public Figures Promote Obesity

Douglas Twenefour

Douglas Twenefour is a dietitian at Central London Community Healthcare in the United Kingdom. In the following viewpoint, Twenefour suggests that celebrities and public figures who embrace being overweight normalize obesity and unhealthy lifestyles. Authority figures are portrayed as "big men" in movies and society, the author continues. He also asserts that in his home country, Ghana, and around the world, fatness is associated with wealth and success, not its dangers to health. Twenefour urges obese stars and leaders to combat their weight problems and to be positive role models for their fans and followers.

As you read, consider the following questions:

1. Why is obesity especially worrisome in Ghana, in the author's view?

Douglas Twenefour, "Health Alert: Obesity, Whose Fault Could It Be Anyway?" *Ghanian Journal*, February 22, 2010. Reproduced by permission.

2. In Twenefour's opinion, how do obese celebrities and leaders present themselves in the media?

3. How should the public look to the famous and public figures, as stated by Twenefour?

I had a conversation with a good friend on my recent return to Ghana. This gentleman had been promoted in his job and was doing well financially, and he was gaining adequate waistline to show for his success. He actually asked to have a chat with me and that got me nervous because he seemed serious about it, only to comment on my weight.

He was wondering if things are okay for me in the UK [United Kingdom] since my weight had stayed stable for well over five years. He did not understand why 'somebody of my position and prestige could be that lean' and was worried because most of our other colleagues come back home 'looking tough'.

It took a lengthy discussion for my 'tertiary' friend to appreciate the fact that someone would make conscious efforts to stay 'lean' in an atmosphere of success and wealth. To him, one needs to show their success and wealth.

It is reasonable to believe that my friend is not isolated in his position. In certain Ghanaian cultures, obesity is seen as a sign of wealth and prestige. In fact, 'potbelly' or 'beer belly' which is medically recognised as the worst form of obesity is adored by certain elite groups as proof of success and achievements.

Adding to the controversies surrounding obesity is the observation that, whereas obesity in industrialised countries is more prevalent within the lower socioeconomic class, it is rather more common within the higher socioeconomic groups in Ghana.

It is incongruous to accept that in Ghana people with tertiary education are presented with the highest levels of obesity compared with the less literate. It is also more prevalent in urban and high-class residences than rural and low-class residences; observations that are also not in conformity with industrialised populations. It is therefore by no coincidence that we observe more chubbiness in the more successful individuals in the Ghanaian society. What is alarming is the fact that these are the same people who are supposed to inspire the next generation of leaders in the country. No wonder the canker [source of debasement] is already being witnessed in some of the 'latter days' leaders.

The 'Big Men' in Society

Take a look at our modern-day politicians, religious leaders, traditional rulers, businessmen, actors and actresses, radio DJs, and presenters, etc., and what you see are individuals who are well content with their bigger frame. And these are the 'big men' in the society. How often do we see 'slim/normal weight' actors made the bosses or the 'big men' in local movies? Perhaps that is a reflection on society, but it is also an indictment on our attitude towards our health and well-being.

Recently, a debate ensued in the UK media regarding the responsibility of chubby celebrities in promoting obesity. As a practising dietitian in the UK, I followed this debate and the discussions generated therein with keen interest.

One can appreciate the assumption that by seeing our chubby 'role models' as often as we do on TVs and other platforms, it fuels the perception that obesity is 'normal' in the eyes of the public. If my MP [member of Parliament] or pastor that I look up to, appears overweight or obese and is content with it; or if my favourite actor/actress is successful with their 'big frame'—then may be it is 'normal'.

Most pastors inspire their congregation to aspire for good things in life, and some cite their achievements as a source of inspiration. These 'vessels of the Lord' hardly lose sight of the fact that they are role models, but they undermine this powerful status by glorifying their huge frame in their pulpits as part of their success stories.

It is inevitable that the public become drawn to their 'role models' especially when they relate to a common factor, in this case being obese or overweight. What could be powerful is if the role model seems to be doing something to reverse this common factor. Unfortunately, hardly do we see any of these leaders promoting healthy lifestyles—instead they prefer to parade on our televisions with their potbellies, round cheeks, hidden/lost necks, etc., all to show off their wealth.

One does not have to look far to appreciate the perceived acceptance and glorification of obesity. A cousin of mine was advised by her fiancé to 'pile up some weight' before their wedding ceremony. To her fiancé, a 'woman must have enough body' and that would be more presentable to his family.

While it would be unacceptable for me to chastise people who are obese/overweight, I have no sympathy for those who make deliberate efforts to be chubby for the wrong reasons. I have been in the business of weight loss/gain long enough to appreciate that it goes beyond health. People make such decisions for all sorts of reasons, and of course, these decisions are theirs to make. Scrutinising these decisions should equally be acceptable to society.

Obesity Is a Disease

To decide to be fat/chubby/flabby/chunky/plump to show off one's success is as absurd as a footballer who celebrates his goal by scoring an own goal [a goal for the other team]. How could increasing one's risk of developing diabetes, heart diseases, strokes, certain types of cancers and premature death be a show off?

Our biggest challenge as a nation lies in our failure to recognise obesity as a disease, and like any other disease should be prevented as much as possible. In Ghana and many middle-income countries, it is not uncommon to find obesity and malnutrition existing in the same community and even the same household.

Whereas we are good at identifying malnutrition as a medical condition that requires expert input, obesity hardly gets attention—because it has become acceptable to the extent that people endeavour to be obese to emulate their 'role models'. In my opinion, aspiring to be as chubby as one's role model is as ludicrous as attempting to go blind because one loves [blind musician] Stevie Wonder.

The public's interest in our politicians, religious leaders, businessmen, actors and actresses should be encouraged. After all, these are successful individuals in our society that people can aspire to be like. However, they should not be perceived as a guide to living our lives. We should tap to their professional minds and achievements, rather than their superficial chubbiness.

Weight-related decisions are better made with particular consideration to our health. People who are less endowed to make such decisions should be guided accordingly. These people should be encouraged to seek appropriate help and supported to make the necessary lifestyle and dietary changes.

Our leaders and 'celebrities' should embrace healthy lifestyle principles and hopefully transfer these to their followers/ 'fans'. They should seek help themselves, and if possible go public about their intentions to seek help and their progress with such help in order to stimulate the minds of their followers/ 'fans' to follow suit. It can not be an acceptable excuse that the responsibilities associated with being a leader or 'celebrity', thwart one's principles of eating healthily and doing more exercise. Indeed, these principles should rather be deepened when one achieves such status—for the benefit of the larger society.

Far from my principles that I would be seen to label blames, but I believe our leaders and 'role models' have a ma-

Expect More of Celebrities

There is a long, star-studded list of athletes, pop idols, and movie icons endorsing food products. There are the obvious ones such as Michael Jordan, Shaquille O'Neal, LeBron James, and Britney Spears, but endorsements of another kind are becoming more and more common. In 2001, for instance, Coca-Cola paid Warner Bros. $150 million for the global marketing rights for the first Harry Potter movie. Appeals to the author of the Harry Potter books (J.K. Rowling) to stop the use of her characters to promote soft drinks to children were unsuccessful.

Why should we not expect more of celebrities? These individuals would probably not endorse cigarette brands, because this could be a public relations disaster, and they might have reservations about promoting products known to cause harm. This is precisely what could happen in the future with endorsements regarding unhealthy foods. Famous people acting as role models, such as LeBron James who signed a $90 million dollar contract with Nike, perhaps through *pro bono* [for the public good] work, could have a positive impact by helping promote healthy foods and physical activity.

Andrew B. Geier and Kelly D. Brownell,
"Acknowledging and Reversing the Toxic Environment,"
Obesity and Cardiovascular Disease. *Eds. Malcom K. Robinson*
and Abraham Thomas. New York:
Taylor & Francis Group, 2006, p. 441.

jor responsibility and a role to play in helping educate the public about their weight in particular and health in general. Obesity should form part of the political discourse, Sunday sermons, radio discussions and education forums. This would help bring the menace to the attention of the Ghanaian public and hopefully disabuse the minds of society from the perception that obesity is ok.

Following the Footsteps

Many industrialised countries have higher levels of obesity than Ghana, but most of them are tackling the problem with their entire armoury. Indeed, obesity and its related conditions are at the centre stage of government policies in many countries. Since we are not that fortunate to have their resources to deal with the problem, I guess we are better off seeking to prevent the problem as much as possible.

Matching trends in our lifestyle, love for technology, attitudes, etc., dictate that we are likely to follow the trend of obesity in industrialised countries—if we do not make concrete efforts to prevent it. We might not possess the financial resources to deal effectively with obesity, but I believe we are endowed with the knowledge and influence from our leaders to help reverse the increase.

My concern is not so much about how reckless our leaders are becoming with their weight and health, but more so about the extent to which the public can go in 'following the footsteps' of these leaders. Their influence continues to be so powerful that, if channelled rightly, this country stands to benefit enormously. It is my ultimate hope that few of them have just chanced on this [viewpoint], and are ready to 'do something about it'—as they often tell us.

Periodical Bibliography

*The following articles have been selected to supplement the
diverse views presented in this chapter.*

Ray Connolly — "The Fatal Attraction of Fame on the Internet That Empowers Twisted, Inadequate Loners," *Daily Mail*, December 9, 2007.

Selwyn Duke — "Michael Jackson and Our Modern Celebrity Culture," *New American*, July 2, 2009.

Kirsty Fairclough — "Fame Is a Losing Game: Celebrity Gossip Blogging, Bitch Culture and Postfeminism," *Genders*, December 2008.

Gregory D. Foster — "A Celebrity Culture in Need of Heroes," CommonDreams.org, July 23, 2006.

Madhukar Kamath — "The Celebrity Culture," *Businessworld*, December 19, 2009.

Dawn Olsen — "Paris Hilton: Celebrity Culture Superhero?" Blogcritics.org, January 26, 2007. http://blogcritics.org.

Matthew Pearl — "Did Charles Dickens' 1867 Trip to America Inspire the First Stirrings of Modern Celebrity Culture?" *Slate*, March 17, 2009.

Maria Russo — "How Celebrity Culture Killed the Oscars," TheWrap.com, February 21, 2009.

Laura Smith — "You Say Celebrity, I Say Culture," *Behind the Spin*, October 11, 2009.

Raymond Tallis — "Stop the Sick, Degrading Culture of Celebrity," *Times* (London), October 14, 2009.

OPPOSING
VIEWPOINTS®
SERIES

CHAPTER 2

How Does Celebrity Culture Affect Young People?

Chapter Preface

Singer and actress Miley Cyrus is the undisputed teen queen in Hollywood. Starting at age thirteen, she translated her titular role in the Disney sitcom *Hannah Montana* into a No. 1 movie, several platinum-selling albums, and a sold-out North American tour. However, as an idol to millions of young girls, her choices and behaviors as a young adult are constantly under scrutiny. In 2008, Cyrus's *Vanity Fair* portrait—in which she clutches a sheet with her back exposed—met with swift disapproval. The next year, her performance at Nickelodeon's Kids' Choice Awards allegedly featured a "pole dance." And in 2010, the star shocked audiences with her revealing stage outfit at the MuchMusic Video Awards, which was publicized in a racy photo distributed by news organization Reuters. "I've just grown up to be this way—it's not like this was me five years ago," the seventeen-year-old told the Associated Press about her mature image. "It's me now, presently."[1]

As Cyrus embarks on a career as a serious recording artist (the last season of *Hannah Montana* wrapped up production in May 2010), some perceive her as leading by negative example. More than 40 percent of teens voted her as the worst role model in a 2009 poll conducted by Web site Just So You Know. In fact, her critics frame her as the "new Britney Spears." Martha Brockenbrough, who writes for Parents' Movie Guide on MSN, claims Cyrus "has even ripped a page from Britney's handbook, publicly proclaiming her virginity while dressing for a hooker convention."[2] Brockenbrough also comments on parents who let their children skip school to see *Hannah Montana: The Movie*. "So, when we know the glitzy teens our children idolize are likely to end up in jail, in rehab,

1. *Montreal Gazette*, June 18, 2010. www.montrealgazette.com.
2. MSN, accessed June 2010. http://movies.msn.com.

or in the grave, why on earth do we go to such lengths to make sure they get to watch their *Hannah Montana*?"

Others, nonetheless, uphold that Cyrus is not as deserving of such criticism. "Cyrus is being criticized because she is very open about her sexuality and sexual feelings in her music," writes journalist Jenny Kobiela-Mondor. "It's really kind of sexist to blast Cyrus for her sexuality as expressed in her music, which is normal for a seventeen-year-old."[3] The authors in the following chapter debate whether or not young people are under the influence of celebrity culture.

3. Fwdailynews.com, June 16, 2010.

| "American teenagers are fixated on fame."

Celebrity Culture Harms Teens

Emily Stimpson

Emily Stimpson is a contributing editor to Our Sunday Visitor, *a Catholic newspaper. In the following viewpoint, Stimpson argues that many American teenagers are obsessed with celebrities and becoming famous, which has negative emotional and social consequences. They do not want fame that is a byproduct of great achievements or contributions, she insists—they want it instantly, without suffering or sacrifice. As a result, Stimpson alleges that youths preoccupied with fame are out of touch with reality, spiritually empty, and unable to appreciate the value of ordinary life. She recommends that parents teach their children self-discipline, humility, and servitude to God.*

As you read, consider the following questions:

1. What did a survey reveal about children and celebrity culture, as described in the viewpoint?

Emily Stimpson, "Fame and Misfortune: Why Teens Thirst for Celebrity in Today's Culture," Our Sunday Visitor, January 11, 2009. Reproduced by permission of the publisher and the author.

2. According to Jake Halpern, how have school curriculums contributed to youths' obsession with fame?

3. As told by the author, how did a French teenager achieve recognition and sainthood?

B lame it on reality TV.

Blame it on the entrenched loneliness of postmodern America.

Blame it on an educational curriculum that was designed to promote self-esteem but ended up overshooting the mark.

Pick your cultural poison. The result remains the same: American teenagers are fixated on fame. More than a third of them would prefer it to beauty, intelligence or strength.

Even more problematic? Those teens aren't just dreaming about being famous: They're planning on it. Thirty-one percent of American teenagers expect they'll be famous one day.

Pipe dream or not, those expectations spell big trouble for the culture now and for years to come.

Easy Way Out

Jake Halpern, author of *Fame Junkies[: The Hidden Truths Behind America's Favorite Addiction]*, discovered that firsthand in 2005, when he attended a convention for aspiring child actors and models.

"I watched mothers from places like Dayton, Ohio, from the heartland of America, scream with excitement as their third-grade daughters strutted across the stage in bikinis. It felt like some weird David Lynch movie," Halpern told *Our Sunday Visitor*. "Kids mistook me for an agent and were throwing themselves at me with wild-eyed desperation. The beggar children of Bombay weren't as fierce or as desperate as some of these kids."

After the convention, Halpern set out to discover whether the children he encountered at the convention were an anomaly. In partnership with Syracuse University, he designed and administered a survey for middle school students to test his suspicions.

The results? Young girls, by a two-to-one margin, would rather be famous than more beautiful. Those same girls, by a margin of three to one, would rather be a personal assistant to a celebrity than a U.S. senator. More than a quarter of the boys and girls surveyed said they believed fame would make them happier and more loved by their families. Most found the idea of dinner with a celebrity like Paris Hilton, Jennifer Lopez or the rapper 50 Cent more appealing than dinner with Jesus Christ.

According to author and professor of English at Providence College Anthony Esolen, the desires of the teens who want to be famous or simply to serve someone who is are rooted in normal healthy desires—the desire for praise and the desire to give one's life in the service of something (or someone) great.

Wanting to be great isn't a terribly unusual or even a terribly bad thing. But the fame for which these teenagers thirst is not the kind of fame that [English poet John] Milton called "the last infirmity of a noble mind"—the fame that comes as a byproduct of doing something great.

"They don't want to conquer Persia," explained Esolen. "They want the glitz and glamour of the mass-media spotlight, even if it's only the reflected spotlight that comes from being near someone famous."

They also want it easy, and they want it fast, with no suffering and no sacrifice. Which is why most fantasize about becoming the next Paris Hilton, not the next Bill Gates.

"The kids want fame in *American Idol* fashion, where one day you're aspiring, the next day you're discovered, and boom, the rules no longer apply to you," said Halpern. "That's a lot more attractive than spending years in your garage developing a microchip."

Spiritual Emptiness

Halpern blames teens' thirst for easy celebrity on a "perfect storm" of cultural problems and technical innovations.

On the technology side, he said, the mass media, which brings entertainment celebrities into homes, grocery stores and schools via tabloids, television and the Internet, bears much of the responsibility.

"Celebrities have become ubiquitous," Halpern explained. "We're much more aware of them than people used to be."

Cable TV and reality TV, he added, have also contributed to the problem, creating more opportunities for people to get their 15 minutes of fame and, accordingly, making the goal of becoming a celebrity seem more realistic.

On a deeper level, Catholic psychologist Dr. Joseph White believes many young people's dreams of fame are a byproduct of their inner loneliness, a loneliness that grows greater by the year as more families fall apart and fewer people have the love, attention and support that traditional family and community relationships provide.

"The average American today has exactly half as many close, deep personal relationships as the average American did 10 years ago," said White. "That's a scary statistic. Fame, and the attention that comes with it, seem like a shortcut to what's gained though deep relationships."

Data from Halpern's survey supports that theory. Teenagers who said they felt lonely some or most of the time were almost twice as likely to see fame as the answer to their problems.

The spiritual emptiness found in so many lives and homes doesn't help either.

"So much of this is rooted in the fear of not being enough," said Ralph Martin, director of the Graduate Program in the New Evangelization at Sacred Heart Major Seminary in Detroit. "People are grasping for love, for attention, for being valued, because they're missing the security that comes from knowing they are eternally loved and valued by God. They're looking for something that is only real, only satisfying when it comes from him."

Great Expectations

That desire may be at the heart of why men and women through the ages, not just now, have dreamt of fame. There is a difference, however, between dreaming of fame and expecting it. And, according to a 2005 study conducted by the *Washington Post*, the Kaiser [Family] Foundation and Harvard University, fame is exactly what 31 percent of American teenagers expect.

That may be the most troubling statistic of all. It corroborates, said Halpern, data from researchers across the country that indicates a growing tendency among American teenagers and young adults toward narcissism, an overweening vanity and self-absorption.

In fact, studies by Keith Campbell at the University of Georgia indicate that on the Narcissism Personality Index, no other demographic group in no other part of the world scores as high as the American teenager.

One culprit for that, said Halpern, may be that the self-esteem curriculums, which have dominated education since the 1970s, have worked a little too well, making people believe not just that they are unique and important, but also that they are more unique and more important than everyone else.

Halpern believes that parents who have a distorted view of what it means to give their children everything don't help, either.

"When I went to the convention, I was expecting to find your typical pushy stage moms," he said. "And I did. But just as often, I came across parents who were completely run by their kid. When you think being a parent means being your kid's personal assistant and chauffeur, it shouldn't be a surprise when your kid ends up being self-centered."

It also shouldn't be a surprise, said White, that teenagers aspire to a form of greatness that comes a little easier than the greatness that came from defeating Napoleon, discovering penicillin or circumnavigating the globe.

"Research from Yale's Child Study Center shows that we have increasing problems with delayed gratification," he explained. "Patience and prudence are virtues we're sorely lacking. We want what we want, and we want it now. People are looking for shortcuts to greatness."

Such shortcuts, however, are costly.

"The person who achieves fame is in deep spiritual danger," Esolen said. "You run the risk of becoming a two-dimensional, cardboard figure, not a real person who is held accountable. And events conspire so that you never wake up to that reality. You never realize that you've lost something of your humanity."

In Touch with Reality

Of course, most young people dreaming about red carpets won't ever walk down one. But their dreams don't come cheap either.

According to White, posting inappropriate pictures on MySpace, broadcasting details of relationships on Facebook, and "twittering" every thought and action are just a few of the ways ordinary teens live out their desire for the spotlight. They treat their own lives like celebrity magazines treat the lives of the stars, shining the spotlight perpetually on themselves.

In that process, said White, "teens sacrifice appropriate boundaries." And the more boundaries teens sacrifice, the more they run the risk of being humiliated and exploited "by information that should have stayed private."

Unrealistic expectations of fame also have consequences that can last long after the demise of Facebook.

"Most of us are not called to be great saints, great leaders, great anything," explained Esolen. "We're just called to be ordinary people doing ordinary things—loving our children, keeping our homes in good repair, walking humbly with our God. That's the way God made us. And he made it so that there is tremendous joy to be derived from the everyday, ordinary world. The more people desire what's not ordinary— fame, celebrity, instant greatness—the less joy they'll find in life."

And the less likely it is that they'll seek after what will bring them that joy.

"To possess the virtue of humility means to be in touch with reality," said Martin. "Ultimately, sanctity is about getting in touch with reality, about understanding who God is and what the purpose of life is."

"The danger of seeking after or expecting fame is that it generates and affirms desires in us that aren't healthy or true," he concluded. "It takes us away from reality. And that reality isn't a burden. Holiness isn't a burden. It's a gift God offers us. That's the purpose for which we were created. And that is the only way we'll ever find true happiness, true joy."

Antidotes to the Fame Bug

How can parents help children set their sights on something other than Hollywood? What's a parent to do once the fame bug bites? Is there an antidote?

Our Sunday Visitor put those questions to Catholic child psychologist Dr. Joseph White and *Fame Junkies* author Jake Halpern. Here's their advice:

Turn off the television: According to the study conducted by Halpern and Syracuse University, teenagers who watch more than five hours of television a day are twice as likely as those who watch less than one hour to prefer fame over beauty, intelligence and strength. They're also twice as likely to believe their families will love them more if they become a celebrity, and much more apt to believe fame is a cure for loneliness.

Ask a different question: "We spend a lot of time asking kids, 'What do you want to do when you grow up?'" said White. "Instead, we need to ask them, 'Who is God calling you to be?'" By promoting the idea of vocation and helping children understand the greatest thing they can do is God's will, White believes parents can direct the innate desire for greatness to its proper end—holiness.

Make kids wait: The allure of Hollywood-style celebrity is rooted in its ease. Halpern described it as "winning the lottery but with more glamour." Accordingly, White advises parents to teach their children that patience, hard work and self-discipline pay off. "It's important to let kids know that we care about them and that we understand waiting is hard," White said. "But it's dangerous to give your child everything they want right when they want it."

Teach children how to make small sacrifices: Whether it's avoiding sweets on Fridays, forgoing a favorite television show or tithing [giving 10 percent to charity, usually the Church] part of their allowance, small sacrifices teach children that giving up something they want a little can help them achieve something they want a lot. According to White, helping children understand "that sometimes we have to make difficult choices to better ourselves," helps them develop the self-discipline they need to grow in holiness, as well as develop deep, lasting relationships.

Encourage children to develop talents in service to God: Whether it's a quick mind, a beautiful voice or a charming personality, all talents are gifts from God and ultimately meant to glorify him. Accordingly, White advises parents to redirect their children's desire to use their talents for fame and glory to instead use them for God. From singing in the choir to evangelizing on a school mission trip, White said activities

"Society is forcing us to grow up too soon. I didn't plan on becoming a train wreck until my mid 20s," cartoon by Marty Bucella. www.CartoonStock.com.

that nurture and direct young people's talents in that way will "help them become the person God made them to be, and find real satisfaction."

"The Last Shall Be First"

God likes doing things a bit backward ... backward, that is, from a human perspective. From his perspective, it's not backward at all—just the way things work in the kingdom of God.

Consider fame.

In the kingdom of man, the way to greatness is to pursue fame and fortune like a predator pursues its prey.

Not so in the kingdom of God. There, the first is last, the last first, the least the greatest and the greatest the least. Littleness, meekness, and poverty carry far more pull than glitz, glamour, and glitter. And the rich have loads more to worry about than the poor. Think "camels" and "eyes of needles."

To make sure the world knows that all that "first last, last first" stuff isn't just talk, God has given the Church thousands of witnesses to the contrary. Those witnesses show the world the way to true greatness, dwarfing seeming giants with sanctified littleness.

The great irony, of course, is that the saints who do that the best, tried so very hard not to. They didn't set out to be great at anything other than following God's will. They didn't plan on teaching the world a lesson. They wanted nobody but God to known their name.

Case in point? St. Anthony of Egypt.

Like many a young man in the fourth century, Anthony spent his days fasting and praying in a hut on the outskirts of his hometown. But, between his neighbors and the demons who paid him regular visits, Anthony found his living situation rather crowded. Retreating across the Nile, the ascetic climbed a mountain, then shut himself into an old fort, determined never to see the face of man again.

That worked for about 20 years. Then, the visitors started arriving. At first, Anthony ignored them, letting their knocks on his door go unanswered. As the knocks grew more persistent, however, Anthony realized he would never get any peace unless he responded to their pleas for guidance in the ascetical life. He emerged from his fort, spent the next five years establishing a colony of monks, then headed off once more into the desert. For the last 45 years of his life, he divided his time between solitude and attending to the pilgrims who relentlessly sought him out.

St. Anthony fruitlessly sought anonymity in the desert. St. Benedict Joseph Labre sought it just as fruitlessly in the city.

The 18th-century French saint journeyed about Europe on foot, seeking to no avail admission to various monasteries and seminaries. Realizing that God was calling him to something else, the young and handsome Benedict became a beggar, wandering from shrine to shrine across western Europe. He finally settled in Rome in 1774. Dressed in rags and sleeping in the streets, he spent most of his days and nights praying before the Eucharist in the churches of the Eternal City.

Growing closer and closer to God, Benedict began manifesting great signs of holiness—levitating, bilocating and even multiplying loaves of bread. Bishops, priests, laymen and laywomen sought him out. Benedict would attend to them, then retreat into obscurity once more. After he died, in the backroom of a butcher shop, all of Rome and half of Italy turned out for his funeral, with the military called in to preserve order.

A century later, a French teenager entered the Carmelite cloister from which she would never emerge. She lived there for less than 10 years, dead at the age of 24 from tuberculosis. The little girl did nothing that the world counts as important. She founded no religious orders, opened no hospitals or schools, traveled to no foreign lands as a missionary. She penned no books for public consumption (although a journal she kept was published posthumously), received no visitors, met with no bishops or princes of the Church. She lived a quiet life filled with prayer, work and the daily offering of suffering. But after Thérèse of Lisieux died, not only was she canonized, but she was also declared a Doctor of the Church and "the greatest saint of modern times."

The man who only wanted to be left alone with God became the Father of Monasticism. The beggar who wanted to spend his days in prayer had his grave visited by tens of thousands of men and women from across Europe. The little girl who wanted to live hidden from the world showed the world the "little way" to God. Those are the types of men and women who fill the kingdom of God—men and women who sought the hidden life, who shunned greatness, and who longed for God's will.

They are men and women who give eternal witness to God's seemingly backward ways.

The Dark Side of Celebrity Obsession

It's one thing for teenagers to dream about fame, but what about the grown-ups? Are they entertaining fantasies of stardom as well?

The answer is no . . . and yes.

Unlike 16-year-olds, most adults know Hollywood won't be calling anytime soon. That doesn't mean, however, that they're any less preoccupied with glitz and glamour than the young ones are. As a culture, Americans are celebrity obsessed.

More than 3.5 million Americans subscribe to *People* magazine. And 1.9 million subscribe to its closest competitor, *US* magazine. Millions more track the ups and downs of their favorite celebrities on top network programs such as *Entertainment Tonight* and *Access Hollywood*, while others tune into the two E! networks on cable—one devoted to what celebrities do, another devoted to what celebrities wear—or log onto the three E! Web sites. There are also hundreds of other fan magazines, Web sites and blog sites—some professional, some very unprofessional—that fill people's seemingly insatiable appetites for news about Brad Pitt, Angelina Jolie and Jen Aniston.

Celebrity "News"

That appetite is, in fact, so big that the network and cable news programs have gotten in the game, regularly devoting more airtime to news about the stars than news about anything else.

In *Fame Junkies*, author Jake Halpern recounts that on Jan. 7, 2005—the day news broke about Aniston and Pitt's divorce—CNN devoted more total coverage to the Aniston/Pitt brouhaha than it did to five other major stories of the day combined—stories about an AIDS research breakthrough, a major White House decision, the Oil for Food scandal, Social Security reform, and espionage in the FBI.

Halpern told *Our Sunday Visitor* that two years later, on a day he was scheduled to talk about the book on CNN, his appearance was cancelled because of breaking news.

The news?

Britney Spears lost custody of her children.

Halpern later went back and did a word count of the news coverage that day. During a 24-hour period, the network devoted almost three times the amount of coverage to the Spears' story as it did to the war in Iraq, and 37 times more coverage to Spears than to the unfolding conflict in Darfur.

"Our obsession with celebrities is distorting our perspective about what's important," said Halpern. "There's a limited amount of space, and celebrity stories push out stories that we could and really should be paying attention to. That's a huge problem."

Losing Perspective

Providence College English professor Dr. Anthony Esolen sees that problem and the obsession causing it as a sign of the spiritual emptiness of contemporary culture, or as Pope Benedict XVI often refers to it, "the anti-culture."

"There's something deeply antithetical to culture itself in this obsession," Esolen explained. "There's a pettiness, a smallness that works against building true culture, which is about heritage, traditions received and devotion to a way of life.

"The more people seek to be fed by mass idols," he continued, "the more they become incapable of appreciating ordinary culture, of making it, remembering it, loving it. We end up becoming fools of the mass market."

And like all those young people obsessed with becoming famous, Esolen added, those simply obsessed with the famous also end up losing their perspective on reality.

"Teenage girls who spend all their time looking at supermodels can no longer appreciate their own beauty, the beauty of an ordinary human body," Esolen said. "Men are infected in the same way. If a celebrity's life becomes your ideal of what a human life should look like, you'll never appreciate the greatness of the human lives around you, including your own."

| "Children are not in nearly as much danger from pop culture as many might fear."

Celebrity and Popular Culture Do Not Harm Young People

Karen Sternheimer

In the following viewpoint excerpted from Connecting Social Problems and Popular Culture: Why Media Is Not the Answer, *Karen Sternheimer maintains that childhood is not under siege by popular culture. Sternheimer argues that violence, substance abuse, and unsafe sex are declining among American youths, despite the potentially bad influences of celebrities, movies, music, and the Internet. She states that media are blamed because they represent the most visible changes in culture, and technology has enabled the young to consume media beyond parental control. Sternheimer is a lecturer in the Department of Sociology at the University of Southern California.*

As you read, consider the following questions:

1. How has childhood changed in the past centuries, according to Sternheimer?

Karen Sternheimer, "Media Phobia #2: Popular Culture Is Ruining Childhood," *Connecting Social Problems and Popular Culture: Why Media Is Not the Answer*. Boulder, CO: Westview Press, 2009, pp. 47, 64–71. Copyright © 2010 Karen Sternheimer. All rights reserved. Reprinted by permission of Westview Press, a member of Perseus Books, L.L.C.

2. In the author's view, what is the real threat to children and adolescents?

3. What is Sternheimer's position on how parents should deal with children's media consumption?

"Pop culture is destroying our daughters," a 2005 *Boston Globe* story declared, affirming what many parents and critics believe. The article, tellingly titled "Childhood Lost to Pop Culture," described young girls "walking around with too much of their bodies exposed," their posteriors visible while sitting in low-rise jeans. The concerns are not just in the U.S. either. A British newspaper warned readers of children's "junk culture," asking whether we have "poisoned childhood" with video games and other kinds of popular culture. A Canadian newspaper asks, "Can the kids be deprogrammed?" noting that "concern is mounting that pop culture may be accountable for a wide range of social and physical problems that begin in childhood and carry through to adulthood."

Stories like these reinforce what many people think is obvious: Childhood is under siege, and popular culture is the main culprit. From celebrities making questionable life choices to violent video games and explicit Web sites, there is certainly a deep well of pop culture to draw from in order to find examples of bad behavior.

But despite the plethora of potential bad influences, children and childhood are not in nearly as much danger from pop culture as many might fear. . . .

The Best Time to Be a Child?

Throughout the past three centuries, childhood has gradually expanded as our economy has enabled most young people to delay entry into the paid labor force. We have also prolonged the time between sexual maturity and marriage, particularly as the onset of puberty happens sooner now for girls than in the past. It is only within the past century that such a large group of physically mature people has had so few rights and responsibilities and been considered emotionally immature, a luxury of prosperity. So while we mourn the early demise of childhood, the reality is that for many Americans, childhood and adolescence have never lasted longer. At the beginning of the twentieth century, a large number of young people entered the labor force and took on many adult responsibilities at fourteen and earlier, compared with eighteen, twenty-one, or even later today. Childhood has been extended chronologically and emotionally, filled with meaning it cannot sustain. Contemporary childhood is charged with providing adults with hope for the future and remembrance of an idealized past. It is a complex and contested concept that adults struggle to maintain to offset anxiety about a changing world.

While the news provides a steady diet of doom-and-gloom reports about young people, on the whole the news is good. High school and college graduation rates are at an all-time high. Youth violence has dropped considerably since the 1990s; the number of homicides involving a juvenile offender fell 65 percent between 1994 and 2002; juvenile crime in general fell nearly 57 percent between 1994 and 2003. The teen birthrate fell 35 percent between 1991 and 2005. According to the Centers for Disease Control and Prevention, fewer teens reported being sexually active in 2007 than in 1991, and those who are used condoms more often. Fewer were involved in fistfights or reported carrying guns in 2007 compared with the early 1990s, and young people were much more likely to wear seat belts and avoid riding in a car driven by a drunk driver. The percentage committing or contemplating suicide decreased steadily as well. . . .

The percentage of high school seniors who report drinking alcohol has been declining annually, as has drinking to intoxication. Rates of both consumption and intoxication are substantially lower than the 1970s and 1980s, when their parents were likely teens. Likewise, illegal drug use has declined since the 1970s and 1980s.

So in spite of public perception and the fears that the new media technologies are breeding a violent, sex-obsessed, hedonistic, and self-indulgent young generation, young people are mostly more sober, chaste, and well-behaved than their parents were or than my generation was in the 1980s. Additionally, nearly 60 percent of teens volunteer, averaging three and a half hours of service each week.

Certainly some changes in the experiences of childhood can be attributed to media and technological changes. For example, cell phones allow kids both greater freedom from and greater contact with parents. Kids can be physically tracked through Global Positioning System (GPS) software embedded in their phones. On the other hand, children can use their phones and the Internet to forge relationships with less parental intervention, but they can also be paged on the playground to return home. And young people do spend a lot of time using new technology.

Although many adults fear that playing video games or using the Internet will harm children, we forget that they also serve to prepare them to participate in a high-tech economy. Visual literacy has become more important in the last fifteen years, as video games and computers became staples in many homes that could afford them. The children we should be worried about are the ones that don't have access to these new technologies.

Changes in childhood may be most apparent when we see kids texting on smart phones while listening to iPods, but technology itself cannot single-handedly create change. The often hidden social conditions that alter experiences of childhood were also behind the creation of these new products; changes in the economy produce both the widespread use of new devices and also specific experiences of childhood. Media technologies are the icons of contemporary society; they represent and reflect what scares us most about the unknown future. We tend to see the most tangible differences and credit them with creating powerful social changes without scratching beneath the surface. To understand changes in childhood we must look further to see more than media.

Childhood Has Not Disappeared

Childhood has not disappeared. Instead it is constantly shifting and mutating with the fluctuations in society. The perceived crisis in childhood is derived from the gap between the fantasy of childhood and the reality. We have filled the idea of childhood with our hopes and expectations as well as our fears and anxieties. We want childhood to be everything adulthood is not, but in reality adults and children live in the same social setting and have more experience in common than adults are often comfortable admitting. Our economic realities are theirs; they suffer when parents lose their jobs, and they feel the effects of political conflicts too. Although we would like to keep the realities of terrorism and violence away from them, unfortunately we cannot. For many young people, these are firsthand experiences, not mediated by television, movies, or popular culture at all.

If childhood has changed it is because the world has changed. Rapid change can be very frightening, even if the changes have many positive outcomes. Social life has been shifting so rapidly in the past few years that yesterday's technological breakthrough is tomorrow's dinosaur, obsolete and useless. Changes in family structure and economic realities render adult control of youth reduced. Automated households rarely require young people to perform lengthy chores to ensure the family's survival, so they are not needed at home as much as they were a few generations ago. And many young people have access to more information now than they did in the past. Yes, this is partially due to media, but it is also a reflection of changing attitudes about sexuality, for example, where open discussion of this topic is much more prevalent than in generations past.

This does not mean that adults should ignore the challenges of childhood—in fact, many of the problems children face are overshadowed by the fear of media. For instance, an up-close look at the roots of problems often blamed on media, like youth violence and teen pregnancy, reveals that poverty, not media, is the common denominator. Poverty, not too much television, creates tangible far-reaching consequences for young people. When communications scholar Ellen Seiter studied adult perceptions of media effects on children, she found that the middle class and affluent were the most likely to blame media for harming children and causing social problems. Lower income people have more experience with the reality of problems like violence to know that the media are not a big part of the equation in their struggles to keep their children safe in troubled communities. Yet our continued response is to attempt to focus on the supposed shortcomings of parents and to see popular culture as childhood enemy number one. Politicians often help us choose to focus on popular culture instead, making it seem like V-chips are more important for children than food stamps and health care.

Ultimately, it is easier to blame media than ourselves for policies that fail to adequately support children. School levies are routinely rejected because we don't want to pay more taxes or don't trust the adults who control school budgets. Affordable, quality child care is so difficult to find because as a society we do not monetarily value people who care for children: Those who do frequently earn less than minimum wage. It is not media that have changed childhood over the past century, it is our changing economy and the reluctance of the public to create programs that deal with the very real challenges children face.

Why We Blame Media Anyway

In spite of the fact that kids today are actually doing quite well by many measures, we worry anyway. Concerns about the next generation are anything but new . . . fearing that the next generation is going downhill is a perennial concern. What is different is that now we have visual manifestations of these fears in the form of all kinds of new media.

In the worrier's defense, many people aren't aware that kids aren't in as much trouble as the news might often detail. And when looking for the source of the alleged problems, we need look no further than what's already in our face: popular culture. It's no wonder, then, that we focus on the most visible changes: In the last century one of the biggest transformations has been the growth of electronic media, which by their very nature command our attention. We have seen the development of movies, television, popular music, video games, and the Internet, each of which has received its share of public criticism. New technologies elicit fears of the unknown, particularly because they have enabled children's consumption of popular culture to move beyond adult control. Parents may now feel helpless to control what music their kids listen to, what movies they see, or what Web sites they visit. Over the past hundred years, media culture has moved from the public sphere (movies) to private (television) to individual (the Internet), each creating less opportunity for adult monitoring.

This is not to say that media content is unimportant, nor am I suggesting that parents ignore their children's media use. These are important family decisions, but on a societal level, media culture is not the root cause of social problems. Media do matter, but not in the way many of us think they do. Communications scholar John Fiske describes media as providing "a visible and material presence to deep and persistent currents of meaning by which American society and American consciousness shape themselves." Media are not the central cause of social change, but they are ever present and reflect these changes, and also bring many social issues to our attention.

Media have become an important American social institution intertwined with government, commerce, family, education, and religion. Communications scholar John Hartley asserts that media culture has replaced the traditional town square or marketplace as the center of social life. He and others argue that it is one of our few links in a large and increasingly segmented society, serving to connect us in times of celebration and crisis in a way nothing else quite can. In a sense, media have become representative of society itself. The media receive the brunt of the blame for social problems because they have become symbolic of contemporary American society.

Media culture also enables young people to develop separate interests and identities from their parents. The biggest complaints I have heard from parents is that their children like toys, music, movies, or television programs that they consider junk, and therefore must have harmful consequences. Listen to yourselves, parents—isn't this exactly what your parents told you about the music you liked? Adults attempt to exercise their power by condemning tastes that differ from their own sensibilities and displace their fears of the future onto popular culture.

Popular culture often reminds us that the myth of childhood innocence cannot be maintained and that knowledge cannot be easily withheld from children. Media threaten to expose the illusion of childhood by revealing things some adults don't want kids to know about, and in some cases by offering content that challenges the wisdom and power of adults. Fears of media power represent displaced fears about social change and changes in childhood.

When we continually focus on media as the Big Bad Wolf devouring childhood, we overlook the historical conditions that shape both the experiences and preferred meaning of childhood. It becomes all too easy to sentimentalize children and childhood rather than understand the complexity of children's experiences. Instead, we often consider young people a potential threat that needs to be controlled, for our safety and theirs. If media can turn some children into cold-blooded killers, as some suspect, then restricting young people's behavior and access to popular culture seems reasonable. We are caught in a contradiction: Children are at once viewed as potential victims in need of protection, too weak and vulnerable to make their own decisions, yet as potential victimizers in need of control, too dangerous to ignore. Fear is a central part of our social construction of childhood.

When we relentlessly pursue the idea that media damage children, we are saying that children are damaged. Adults have always believed that kids were worse than the generation before, dating back to Socrates in ancient Greece, who complained about children's materialism, manners, and general disrespect for elders. Blaming the media is much like attempting to swim full force against a powerful riptide: You end up exhausted and frustrated and get nowhere. Understanding what is really happening will allow the swimmer to survive. Likewise, projecting our collective concern about both childhood and society onto media will not take us very far. It will force us to focus on only a small part of the equation and ultimately drive a wedge between generations.

> "One thing is not in doubt: A lot of parents are wondering about the effect our racy popular culture may have on their kids and the women they would like their girls to become."

Celebrities Are Poor Role Models for Young People

Kathleen Deveny

In the following viewpoint, Kathleen Deveny states that young people are at risk of mimicking the out-of-control behavior of their favorite celebrities. Deveny cites a Newsweek *poll in which the majority of Americans believe female celebrities like Lindsay Lohan and Britney Spears have too much influence on young girls. To counter the poor role models these celebrities present, the author advises the parent to step in and take control. Attentive parents and friends can act as an excellent counterbalance to the promiscuous celebrity spectacles. Deveny is deputy editor and global business editor for* Newsweek *magazine and occasionally writes parenting columns for the magazine.*

Kathleen Deveny, "Girls Gone Bad: Paris, Britney, Lindsay & Nicole: They Seem to Be Everywhere and They May Not Be Wearing Underwear. Tweens Adore Them and Teens Envy Them. But Are We Raising a Generation of 'Prosti-Tots'?" *Newsweek*, February 12, 2007. Reproduced by permission.

As you read, consider the following questions:

1. The author states that it's a struggle to impart the right values to kids. What "ancient role of warfare" does she say applies?

2. The affair of what actress "scandalized" America in 1962?

3. Does the author believe that the appalling antics of celebrities can be teachable moments for parents?

My 6-year-old daughter loves Lindsay Lohan. Loves, loves, *loves* her. She loves Lindsay's hair; she loves Lindsay's freckles. She's seen *The Parent Trap* at least 10 times. I sometimes catch her humming the movie's theme song, Nat King Cole's "Love." She likes *Herbie Fully Loaded* and now we're cycling through *Freaky Friday*. So when my daughter spotted a photo of Lindsay in the *New York Post* at the breakfast table not long ago, she was psyched. "That's Lindsay Lohan," she said proudly. "What's she doing?"

I couldn't tell her, of course. I didn't want to explain that Lindsay, who, like Paris Hilton and Britney Spears, sometimes parties pantyless, was taking pole-dancing lessons to prepare for a movie role. Or that her two hours of research left her bruised "everywhere." Then again, Lindsay's professional trials are easy to explain compared with Nicole Richie's recent decision to stop her car in the car-pool lane of an L.A. freeway. Or Britney Spears's "collapse" during a New Year's Eve party in Las Vegas. Or the more recent report that Lindsay had checked into rehab after passing out in a hotel hallway, an item that ran on the *Post*'s Page Six opposite a photo of Kate Moss falling down a stairway while dressed in little more than a fur jacket and a pack of cigarettes.

Oversexed, Underdressed Celebrities

Something's in the air, and I wouldn't call it love. Like never before, our kids are being bombarded by images of oversexed, underdressed celebrities who can't seem to step out of a car without displaying their well-waxed private parts to photographers. Videos like *Girls Gone Wild on Campus Uncensored* bring in an estimated $40 million a year. And if *Us* magazine, which changed the rules of mainstream celebrity journalism, is too slow with the latest dish on "Brit's New Man," kids can catch up 24/7 with hugely popular gossip blogs like perezhilton.com, tmz.com or defamer.com.

Allow us to confirm what every parent knows: kids, born in the new-media petri dish, are well aware of celebrity antics. But while boys are willing to take a peek at anyone showing skin, they're baffled by the feuds, the fashions and faux pas of the Brit Pack. Girls, on the other hand, are their biggest fans. A recent *Newsweek* poll found that 77 percent of Americans believe that Britney, Paris and Lindsay have too much influence on young girls.

Hardly a day passes when one of them isn't making news. Paris Hilton "was always somewhere, doing something," says Melissa Monaco, an 18-year-old senior at Oldfield's boarding school for girls in Maryland, who describes herself as a recovered Paris Hilton addict. "I loved everything from her outfits to her attitude," she says. And it's not just teenagers. Julie Seborowski, a first-grade teacher at Kumeyaay Elementary School in San Diego, says she sees it in her 7-year-old students: girls using words like "sexy," singing pop songs with suggestive lyrics and flirting with boys.

That's enough to make any parent cringe. But are there really harmful long-term effects of overexposure to Paris Hilton? Are we raising a generation of what one L.A. mom calls "prosti-tots," young girls who dress like tarts, live for Dolce & Gabbana purses and can neither spell nor define such words as "adequate"? Or does the rise of the bad girl signal something more profound, a coarsening of the culture and a devaluation of sex, love and lasting commitment? We're certainly not the first generation of parents to worry about such things, nor will we be the last. Many conservative thinkers view our sex-drenched culture as dangerous; liberals are more prone to wave off fears about the chastity of our daughters as reactionary. One thing is not in doubt: A lot of parents are wondering about the effect our racy popular culture may have on their kids and the women they would like their girls to become. The answers are likely to lie in yet another question: Where do our children learn values?

Learning Values at Home

Here's a radical idea—at home, where they always have. Experts say attentive parents, strong teachers and nice friends are an excellent counterbalance to our increasingly sleazy culture. Statistical evidence indicates that our girls are actually doing pretty well, in spite of Paris Hilton and those like her: Teen pregnancy, drinking and drug use are all down, and there is no evidence that girls are having intercourse at a younger age. And in many ways it's a great time to be a girl: Women are excelling in sports, academics and the job market. It's just that the struggle to impart the right values to our kids is a 24/7 proposition. It can be done, but an ancient rule of warfare applies: First, know thy enemy.

"It takes a very strong adolescent to know what's right and what's wrong and not get sucked into all this stuff," says Emily Waring, 40, a paralegal from San Diego and mother of two girls, ages 9 and 2. Waring says her "mom radar" is always on because she believes negative influences, including entertainers like Britney Spears, are everywhere. "Kids can so easily stray," she says.

Nobody wants her bright, innocent girls to grow up believing "hard-partying heiress" is a job title to which they can aspire. But does dressing like Paris or slavishly following the details of Britney's love life make kids more likely to stray? Educators say they don't believe most girls in middle school wear short skirts or midriff shirts to attract the attention of older men, or even boys. (High school is, granted, a different story.) Sixth graders dress to fit in with other girls and for acceptance in social groups. "They dress that way because that's what they see in the media," says Nancy T. Mugele, who works in communications at Roland Park Country School in Baltimore. "They don't want to be different." ...

The Decline of Hollywood Role Models

By the '50s, both Hollywood and the public took a harsh view of female stars' off-screen indiscretions. In 1950, Ingrid Bergman was America's sweetheart, having starred in *The Bells of St. Mary's* and *Notorious*. But when Bergman, then married, had an affair with director Roberto Rossellini, who was also married, and gave birth to their child, she was shunned by Hollywood and called "a powerful influence for evil" on the floor of the Senate. (Hollywood "forgave" Bergman a few years later by giving her an Oscar for *Anastasia*.) After news broke that Marilyn Monroe would be featured in a nude calendar, Hollywood proclaimed her career DOA. (She was on the cover of *Life* magazine a month later, and went on to the biggest roles of her career.)

America was scandalized in 1962 when Elizabeth Taylor cheated on Eddie Fisher with Richard Burton during the filming of *Cleopatra*. The Vatican denounced her as "a woman of loose morals." When "Dickenliz," as they were known, checked into a Toronto hotel, protesters marched outside with signs that read DRINK NOT THE WINE OF ADULTERY, according to a 1964 *Newsweek* article. But soon America's priorities shifted. The Vietnam War was on television; the civil rights movement was in the streets, and the national mood had been sobered by the assassinations of John F. Kennedy, Martin Luther King Jr. and Robert Kennedy. The '60s also brought reliable contraception in the form of the birth control pill and ushered in the sexual revolution. We no longer needed to look to Hollywood for bad influences; the girl next door, the one with birth control pills and a couple of joints tucked into her fringed purse, became the new object of our anxiety.

America had become harder to shock—until 1984, that is, when Madonna showed up in a wedding dress at the first MTV Video Music Awards and sang "Like a Virgin" while writhing on the floor. When her "Virgin" tour opened a year later, parents fretted over the hordes of Madonna wannabes who thronged her concerts dressed in tatty lace, spandex and armfuls of black rubber bracelets. The Material Girl went on to outrage both Planned Parenthood and the Catholic Church in 1986 with her single "Papa Don't Preach," about a pregnant teenager. The 1992 coffee-table book called *Sex*, which glorified nearly every sexual fetish you can think of, cemented her title as the Queen of Bad Girls. Eleven years later she passed on her crown to Britney with a lingering French kiss on the stage of yet another MTV Video Music Awards ceremony. . . .

Under Parents' Control

And as much as we hate to admit it, we grown-ups are complicit. We're uncomfortable when kids worship these girls, yet we also love *Us* magazine; we can't get enough of YouTube videos or "E! True Hollywood Stories." So rather than wring our hands over an increase in 17-year-olds getting breast implants, what if we just said no? They're minors, right? And while we worry that middle schoolers are dressing like hookers, there are very few 11-year-olds with enough disposable income to keep Forever 21 afloat. The greatest threat posed by these celebrity bad girls may be that they're advertising avatars, dressed by stylists and designers, who seem to live only to consume: clothes, cell phones, dogs and men. But there's good news: that problem is largely under the control of we who hold the purse strings.

And even if our adolescents pick up a few tricks from the Brit Pack, we have a big head start on them. We begin to teach our kids values while they're still in diapers. "Kids learn good morals and values by copying role models who are close to them," says Michele Borba, author of *Building Moral Intelligence*. Experts say that even the most withdrawn teens scrutinize their parents for cues on how to act. So watch your behavior; don't gossip with your friends in front of the kids and downplay popularity as a lifetime goal. Parents need to understand and talk about the things that interest their kids—even if it's what Paris is wearing—without being judgmental. That makes it easier for kids to open up. "The really subtle thing you have to do is hear where they are coming from, and gently direct them into thinking about it," says Borba. That means these celebrities gone wild and all their tabloid antics can be teachable moments. Lesson No. 1: wear underwear.

> "When choosing role models, the teens surveyed said the most important qualities they look for include biblical principles such as honesty, integrity, loyalty and truthfulness."

Many Young People Do Not Look to Celebrities as Role Models

PR Newswire

The following viewpoint discusses a survey in which the data dispels the popular thought that teenagers primarily look to celebrities and athletes as role models. In a survey conducted by the American Bible Society, teens named parents, teachers, and coaches as their main role models and heroes. The viewpoint claims that teens look for heroes that are within reach and with whom they have regular interactions. PR Newswire is a leading global vendor in information and news distribution services for professional communicators.

As you read, consider the following questions:

1. What "biblical principles" does the viewpoint claim teens look for in role models?

2. Who were the "most frequently cited role models among religious leaders"?

3. According to the viewpoint, what percentage of teens has considered biblical figures as role models?

Dispelling the conventional wisdom that celebrities, athletes and entertainers are the primary role models teenagers look to most, a survey conducted by the American Bible Society revealed that 67.7% of 12–18-year-olds believe parents are the most important role models in today's society. When choosing role models, the teens surveyed said the most important qualities they look for include biblical principles such as honesty, integrity, loyalty and truthfulness. More than 1,100 12–18-year-olds participated in an eight-question survey conducted by Weekly Reader Research on behalf of the American Bible Society.

Who are teens' role models and heroes?

Teens today have many role models to choose from and this survey reveals the following information:

—After parents, 40.6% said teachers and coaches followed by siblings (40.4%), religious leaders (18.7%), athletes (18.3%), and celebrities (16.5%);

—27.5% of African American teens said religious leaders are role models compared to 17.3% of Caucasian teens;

—25% of African American teens said athletes are role models compared to 16.7% of Caucasian teens;

—84.8% of teens selected Jesus as the embodiment of a biblical role model.

The survey also discovered that teens today look for role models and heroes within their reach and who they have regular interaction with and access to. In open-ended questioning, the most frequently cited role models among religious leaders were "my priest," "my pastor," or "Father Tom," followed by Jesus, the pope, God, the Prophet Mohammed and Billy Graham.

"We are delighted to see that such a significant number of teens in our society today have biblical heroes, in addition to the role models provided by parents and religious leaders in their circles of interaction," said Dr. Paul Irwin, president and CEO of the American Bible Society. "This is a confirmation of the relevance of the Bible in the lives of today's young people."

The Bible's Influence

In additional opened-ended questioning, the most frequently cited biblical role models, in addition to Jesus, were Moses, Joseph, Mary, Paul, and Esther. Religious figures that are not in the Bible, such as Buddha, the Prophet Mohammed, and Joseph Smith were also listed by the respondents as role models.

The survey also examined the Bible's influence on teenagers when choosing role models/heroes:

—46.8% of teens have considered biblical figures as role models;

—A significantly greater number of African American teens (65.9%) than Caucasian (44.2%) or Hispanic teens (36.5%) have considered biblical figures as role models.

The Role of Pop Culture Icons

In a series of open-ended questions, teens were asked to write in names of famous people they see as role models today.

—Most frequently cited celebrity role models: Angelina Jolie, Oprah Winfrey, Beyoncé [Knowles], Hilary Duff and Kanye West.

—Most frequently cited athlete role models: Michael Jordan, Shaun Alexander, Lance Armstrong, Mia Hamm, and David Beckham.

—Most frequently cited political role models: Barack Obama, Hillary Clinton, George Bush, and Bill Clinton.

—Most frequently cited business role models: Bill Gates, Donald Trump, Russell Simmons, Oprah Winfrey, and Steve Jobs.

When asked if they consider themselves a role model for others, 40% of teens said yes and 23% said no while 37% did not know.

—Of those teens who said yes, 51% have a biblical role model.

—55% of African American teens said they consider themselves to be role models compared to 38% of Caucasian teens.

The survey also revealed these newfound statistics:

—63.7% of America's teens aged 12–18 have heroes or role models.

—22.3% of all teens said honesty is the most important trait for a role model. 76.1% of girls said loyalty is an important quality while only 63.8% of boys agree.

The study was representative of U.S. population of teens. The participants were 79% Caucasian, 14% African American, 16% Hispanic/Latino, 4% Asian, 2% Native American, and overall the participants were 51% male and 49% female. The results are based on Internet surveys, which were conducted between January 19 and 22, 2007. The maximum margin of sampling error is plus or minus 2.8 percentage points. In addition to sampling error, question wording and practical difficulties in conducting surveys can introduce error or bias into the findings of public opinion polls.

Periodical Bibliography

The following articles have been selected to supplement the diverse views presented in this chapter.

Margaret Bernstein   "Does Reality TV for Teens Induce Bad Behavior?" Cleveland.com, March 18, 2008.

Kathy Brewis   "Suicide: A Teen's Way to Instant Fame," *Sunday Times* (London), January 27, 2008.

Katharine DeBrecht   "Kids Mimicking Celebs' Debauchery?" WorldNetDaily.com, July 26, 2006. www.wnd.com.

Sharon Jayson   "Celebrity Narcissism: A Bad Reflection for Kids," *USA Today*, March 16, 2009.

Corey Kilgannon   "Teenagers Misbehaving, for All Online to Watch," *New York Times*, February 13, 2007.

Melanie Lindner   "Teen Celebrity Entrepreneurs," *Forbes*, May 28, 2009.

Danny Miller   "American Teen: The Downside of 'Reality,'" *Huffington Post*, July 30, 2008.

Susan Smith Nash   "Does Our 'e-Celebrity' Culture Affect e-Learning?" E-Learning Queen, September 20, 2007. http://elearnqueen.blogspot.com.

Stephanie Emma Pfeffer   "What Teens Can Learn from Celebrity Scandals," *Family Circle*, March 2010.

Rebecca Traister   "Return of the Brainless Hussies," *Salon*, May 16, 2006.

CHAPTER 3

Does Celebrity Activism Benefit Society?

Chapter Preface

The late Diana, Princess of Wales, was well renowned for her charity work. "Diana used her power just like a magic wand, waving it in all kinds of places where there was hurt,"[1] said Debbie Tate, cofounder of Grandma's House, a shelter for HIV-positive children. For instance, Diana is credited with dispelling the misconception that the virus was spread through casual contact when she held the hand of an AIDS patient in April 1987. The "People's Princess" also played a key role in 120 countries signing an anti-landmine treaty by visiting Angola—dressed in protective gear—to observe efforts to remove the explosives in February 1997. "She redefined the way famous people got involved in political issues,"[2] claimed Rachel Giese, a Canadian arts writer. "Diana didn't just lend her visage or show up at a benefit. She got her hands dirty in the field, and she sat down at the table with leaders and activists."

Diana, however, had her share of detractors. Her friend, Tina Brown, former editor of the *New Yorker* and *Vanity Fair*, wrote devastating claims about her in *The Diana Chronicles*. According to Brown, Diana was a "spiteful, manipulative, media-savvy neurotic" who allegedly timed her philanthropic activities to draw media attention away from Prince Charles. A friend of Brown, discussing the biography, stated, "Diana was a humanitarian who at one level really identified with the common people, as she thought of them. But she was also a very messed-up woman whose downfall was due to her own insane jealousy and self-obsession."[3]

More than a decade after her death, Diana still serves as the case study for modern celebrity philanthropy—to both its

1. *People*, February 2, 1998. www.people.com.
2. cbc.ca, June 27, 2007. www.cbc.ca.
3. *Mail Online*, April 24, 2007. www.dailymail.co.uk.

proponents and opponents. In the following chapter, the authors examine the impacts and motivations of political activism and charity among celebrities.

| "America's obsession with the glitterati can be extremely useful to nonprofit organizations."

Celebrity Activism Can Be Beneficial

Kate Bowman Johnston

In the following viewpoint, Kate Bowman Johnston writes that celebrities can help boost humanitarian efforts and charitable causes. Hollywood figures and rock icons, she asserts, bring issues into the limelight and to the attention of the fickle public, and organizations harness star power to increase public awareness, media interest, and political influence. While critics maintain that celebrities lack the clout of elected officials and are not accountable to a broader movement, the author suggests that the awareness they bring to crises around the world is still beneficial. Bowman Johnston is the children's librarian at the Chestnut Hill Branch of the Free Library in Philadelphia, Pennsylvania.

As you read, consider the following questions:

1. How did star power bring more attention to the crisis in Darfur, in the author's view?

Kate Bowman Johnston, "Celebrity Activists," *Sojourners Magazine*, July 2006, pp. 38, 41–43. Copyright © 2006 Sojourners. Reproduced with permission from Sojourners. (800) 714-7474, www.sojo.net.

2. How have nongovernmental organizations "gone big," as stated by the author?

3. Why does Marie Clarke Brill object to placing celebrities at the front of humanitarian campaigns?

An aid-worker friend in Darfur has sent e-mail updates during the past year [2006] about the escalating crisis there. They often included the worried questions: "Is this on the radar in the States? Does anyone care?"

I always answered, sadly, that despite some notable exceptions (*New York Times* columnist Nicholas Kristof for one), Sudan largely went unmentioned in the mainstream press—that is, until mid-May of this year, when the issue consistently made it into the headlines. According to the Associated Press, the three network evening newscasts had devoted less than a combined 10 minutes to the conflict in 2006—and in under a week, that airtime skyrocketed. Suddenly, everyone was talking about Darfur.

Why? Certainly years of activist work was finally paying off. But another factor was star power. Actor George Clooney traveled to a Sudanese refugee camp armed with a video camera and his celebrity, then returned to speak at a well-attended rally in Washington, D.C. Meanwhile, NBC's medical drama *ER* aired a special episode featuring two attractive doctors getting their hands dirty in the African nation, with the actors appearing on news magazine shows to speak about the crisis.

Clooney and the *ER* docs aren't alone. Chances are that by the time you read this, several other international hot spots will have had their moment in the limelight—thanks to a phenomenon *Time* columnist James Poniewozik calls "charitainment." In Hollywood, it seems, philanthropy is the new black. From Meg Ryan to Angelina Jolie to the ubiquitous Bono, A-listers are promoting a slew of humanitarian causes, from the fight against AIDS to the alleviation of Third World debt to trade justice issues, fueled by the knowledge that, as

Poniewozik notes wryly, "in this world, nothing matters that does not have a camera pointed at it."

Obviously, celebrity activism isn't new; think of [actress] Audrey Hepburn's tenure as a UNICEF [United Nations Children's Fund] goodwill ambassador, or the string of musical benefits kicked off by George Harrison's 1971 Concert for Bangladesh. But the recent spate of celebrity activism is distinctive in its scale. For example, possibly hundreds of prominent actors, musicians, athletes, and other entertainers have signed on to support the ONE Campaign. These days, celebrities are in the news as much for exposure trips to distant lands as for the usual vapid exploits. Whether or not this is good for activism is the subject of much debate among those working on the ground.

Providing Charities with Visibility

The demand for celebrity sponsorship is energized by the millennial mandate to "go big" when it comes to political organizing. In contrast to a traditionally grassroots approach, many nongovernmental organizations—weary of being sidelined or overlooked—have banded together to form social justice super-alliances. Coalitions such as the ONE Campaign (and its U.K. [United Kingdom] counterpart, Make Poverty History) act as umbrellas for dozens of independent groups, providing them not only with improved access to resources but to organizing's Holy Grail: Visibility. A coalition like ONE works because it is too massive to ignore.

Visibility is the watchword for today's organizations, as they seek to fix the short attention spans of a fickle public on issues they might otherwise consider boring, irrelevant, or too overwhelming to tackle. "Politicians don't really have to address [debt or trade] because the issue isn't in the public domain," says Glen Tarman, coordinator for Britain's Trade Justice Movement and a cofounder of Make Poverty History. "The reality is that unless you get your issue out of the business pages and into the broader media, you won't build the climate for change. It's just an absolute reality of the modern age."

And nothing catapults issues into the public consciousness like a famous face—preferably a sexy one with a well-documented history in the tabloids. As political satirist Stephen Colbert has joked of celebrity activism, "Brangelina [actors Brad Pitt and Angelina Jolie] is raising awareness of the Darfur situation, but he/she also has the courtesy to captivate us with his/her baby bump." But despite the bizarre juxtaposition of the realities of poverty with what passes for reality in Hollywood, America's obsession with the glitterati can be extremely useful to nonprofit organizations. As Claire Lewis of Oxfam says, "Celebrities can turn something that is an issue in boardrooms and grey-suited meetings into a water-cooler moment and bring these subjects into cafés and pubs."

Jennifer Coulter Stapleton, a spokesperson for founding ONE member Bread for the World, based in Washington, D.C., agrees. "I'm not sure why we're so fascinated with celebrities, or why people listen to them—but I know that we do," she says. "So as a person who's trying to move people toward the movement to overcome hunger, then I have to recognize that and use that in every way I can. And God bless the celebrities for letting me."

Organizations such as ONE and Make Poverty History typically divide the benefits of celebrity endorsement into three categories: increased public awareness, increased media interest, and increased political influence. The organizations I surveyed all reported spikes in Web-based responses and attendance at events when a celebrity became involved; Brad Pitt's televised trip to Africa last year with Diane Sawyer meant that in-boxes overflowed with millions of inquiries and signatures to ONE's petition. This response is especially typical of young people, whom organizers usually have trouble engaging. As Oxfam's Lewis notes, 84 percent of British 16- to 24-

year-olds who were questioned about the Make Trade Fair campaign knew about it from a rock star, Coldplay's Chris Martin.

Mainstream media outlets are also more likely to bite on a justice story if there's a Hollywood worm on the hook. Stapleton says that when she pitches Bono to an editor, she gets "two more minutes" than if she were simply pitching Bread for the World. Similarly, Tarman chuckles over a story his Make Poverty History group was trying to get into the *Financial Times*. "[They] weren't interested. But when we offered them [alternative rock band] Radiohead, even a serious newspaper . . . said they'd love to come and interview Radiohead! And Radiohead spoke about trade justice in a newspaper that would normally just feature CEOs [chief executive officers] and the usual business columnists."

Strange Bedfellows

Politicians don't appear immune to celebrity charm, either. When asked what they thought of the 2005 Make Poverty History campaign, British government ministers said "they couldn't ignore it, because it wasn't just the campaign groups, it was all these public figures," Tarman says. "They're actually scared of the agenda when so many celebrities are involved." Not so scared, however, that they're unwilling to open their doors to actors or musicians; many of them are invited in for conversations activists wouldn't be. Tarman said singer-songwriter Bob Geldof was able to work a trade justice clause into British Prime Minister Tony Blair's Commission for Africa, ensuring that trade liberalization would not be forced on poor countries. "We wouldn't have gotten that in," Tarman says. "We as activists wouldn't have been invited onto the commission."

This is where celebrity organizing becomes unsavory. What does it mean that decision makers can, to use Poniewozik's only slightly hyperbolic example, "ignore [former secretary-

A Gold Standard

[U2 singer] Bono used the leverage of fame in a way that few stars had before. He studied the issues, and he lobbied not just U.S. representatives but their aides. He approached [Microsoft chairman and philanthropist] Bill Gates and George Soros [Hungarian businessman and philanthropist], whose vast wealth has enabled them to become central figures in the world of advocacy, and made them his partners. He became a roving ambassador for Africa, traveling there frequently. And he shouldered his way into the places where the world's most consequential decisions are made—Davos [Switzerland at the meeting of the World Economic Forum], the G-8 [a forum for the representatives of eight countries], the World Bank, 10 Downing Street [home of the British prime minister] and the White House. Bono offered decision makers an implicit bargain: Do the right thing, and I'll say so in public. His currency was not just his fame but his credibility. Bono made himself into such a gold standard that the White House insisted he stand with President [George W.] Bush in March 2002, when Bush announced the Millennium Challenge Account, his signature initiative on foreign aid.

James Traub, "The Celebrity Solution,"
New York Times, March 9, 2008.

general of the UN] Kofi Annan all you want, but blow off Lara Croft at your peril"? That entertainers are accepted into the inner circles, while those doing the work on the ground and in the streets are brushed aside?

Organizers agree that Hollywood and activism can make for strange bedfellows. Stapleton emphasizes that celebrity can't be an end unto itself; she says it's her job to engage constituents substantively and involve them for the long haul. Tarman admits that "some of the glossy magazines seem very, very strange when you've got one page with what's going on [in the world], and then [advertising] from the very corporations that are lobbying governments to create trade injustices."

Some nonprofits find the trend of celebrity activism so problematic they've opted out of it entirely. Africa Action, for example, is a small but influential Washington, D.C.-based group that has played an important role in addressing the Darfur crisis by pushing for a multinational peacekeeping intervention. They deliberately chose not to join the ONE Campaign so they could focus a strong, nuanced message to their largely African-American and African-diaspora constituency.

Marie Clarke Brill, who directs public education and mobilizing for the group, says that "the closer you get to decision makers, the more likely you are to make compromises. The challenge of that dynamic with a celebrity making those compromises is that the celebrity has not been elected by anyone, nor are they accountable to a broader movement of people working on that issue."

Brill also rejects the utilitarian argument for putting celebrities at the helm of humanitarian campaigns. "As activists working for justice and peace, we look at our system today, and we say it's not acceptable—and we work to change that system," she says. "I think it's the same thing when it comes to celebrities. Just because it works doesn't mean it's the best way to work. We need to start to organize in the way we would like to see power be distributed in the world."

For Brill, this means privileging sustained, systemic change over initial numeric success or compromised victories. "At the end of the day, if we are going to be successful at achieving justice and peace, we need to be able to build a different culture in our country—one that really values the basic dignity of human life and understands that our liberation is connected to the liberation of people around the world."

Of course, sometimes that dignity begins with affirming that a previously neglected person does, in fact, exist. "I wish I could bring everyone out here to see it all for themselves," Oxfam's Lewis laments. "No one with a heart could fail to be moved by Africa and see that something has to be done." In that sense, perhaps it's a good thing that all over the world, cameras are swinging toward the people of Darfur—even if it took a handsome white celebrity to convince them to focus there. Time will tell if the American public can get its collective nose out of *People* magazine long enough to be captivated by the dignity of very real, ordinary, lowercase-p people.

> "Rather than raising the ability of Africans to help themselves, celebrity campaigns may well lead the continent into ever deeper trouble."

Celebrity Activism Is Not Beneficial

Heribert Dieter and Rajiv Kumar

Heribert Dieter and Rajiv Kumar challenge celebrity activism and humanitarian efforts in the following viewpoint. They contend that celebrities' well-meaning interventions and campaigns to end hunger and poverty in Africa are overly simplistic and fail to enable impoverished nations and peoples to help themselves. The authors argue that stability and growth depend on improving governance and leadership in Africa, and activists must be less paternalistic and more attuned to the complexities of development and diplomacy. Dieter is a senior fellow at the German Institute for International and Security Affairs. Kumar is director of the Indian Council for Research on International Economic Relations.

As you read, consider the following questions:

1. How do Dieter and Kumar describe Bono's clout?

2. Why are the authors skeptical of Jeffrey Sachs?

3. What concern do Dieter and Kumar raise about Debt AIDS Trade Africa (DATA)?

Celebrities have become important participants in the debate on the future of development. The Irish rock star Paul Hewson, better known as Bono, is not only the front man of the band U2 but has also become the champion of an antipoverty movement with worldwide impact. Bono is supported by US economist Jeffrey Sachs, who has become a global spokesperson for poverty reduction, especially in Africa.

Surprisingly, the recipes being suggested by Bono and Sachs are breathtakingly one-dimensional and akin to the sweeping propositions of the 1960s: Give aid to Africa, waive debt, and provide education, and the continent will develop. While these remedies may look seductive, unfortunately the reality is far more complex and demands attention to the specific circumstance of each individual country or subregion. Grand ideas for development are a dangerous recipe and may in fact worsen the situation of the poor.

In this [viewpoint] we address three issues related to the role of celebrities in international relations. First, we chart the rise of prominent celebrity activists in international affairs, in particular their impact on development policies of the member countries of the Organisation for Economic Co-operation and Development (OECD). Second, we examine the competence of celebrities to handle development issues and suggest a more nuanced and less paternalistic approach. Third, we consider the legitimacy of celebrity activists and whether these nonelected individuals are well positioned to berate democratically elected governments.

Celebrities in Politics

At the beginning of the twenty-first century, development policy is heavily influenced, in the words of [economics professor] Paul Collier, by development biz and development buzz. Development biz encompasses the aid bureaucracies, aid agencies, and development nongovernmental organizations (NGOs), all of whom make a living out of development. Development buzz, for its part, comes from rock stars, celebrities, and NGOs.

Development buzz has been a door opener for Bono and other celebrities in recent years. In 1999, Bono had an audience with Pope John Paul II. Six years later, *Time* magazine named Bono, together with Melinda and Bill Gates [Microsoft chairman and philanthropist], as "Persons of the Year." Bono has attended the World Economic Forum in Davos [Switzerland] as well as several summits of the Group of 8 (G-8) [a forum for eight countries to meet]. He and fellow activist Bob Geldof gained particular prominence at the Gleneagles G-8 summit of 2005 and the Heiligendamm G-8 summit of 2007. At Gleneagles, Bono had one-on-one meetings with George W. Bush, [British prime minster] Tony Blair, [German politician and one-time chancellor of Germany] Gerhard Schröder, and [Canadian prime minister] Paul Martin and also met [French president] Jacques Chirac after the summit. At Heiligendamm, Bono again claimed center stage, holding meetings with various leading politicians. His supporters even set up camp in Berlin months before the event.

The attention celebrity diplomats received surrounding Heiligendamm was overwhelming. For example, for its May 2007 edition, *Vanity Fair* had a German singer, Herbert Grönemeyer, as its guest editor, and dozens of celebrities expressed their concern about poverty and hunger. Concurrently Bob Geldof was guest editor of an issue of the German tabloid *Bild-Zeitung* that laced pleas for greater development assistance with pictures of dying children and people afflicted with AIDS.

Efficient public relations work has made celebrities core players who had better be consulted. Politicians today can hardly avoid meetings with Bono. When Stephen Harper, Canadian prime minister, said he was too busy for a meeting with Bono during the Heiligendamm summit, the rock star did not take no for an answer. He growled that Harper had blocked progress on aid for Africa, and the intimidated prime minister promised to find time for a meeting.

Celebrity diplomacy extends well beyond G-8 meetings and development issues, of course. [Actor] George Clooney pronounces on Darfur. [Actor/director] Robert Redford pronounces on Iraq. Not everyone is impressed. For example, Gideon Rachman of the *Financial Times* castigates Bono as "a grandstanding poseur who has intimidated blameless bankers and politicians into taking him seriously by sheer force of celebrity." In any case, the phenomenon of celebrity activism in international affairs has become too serious to be ignored.

Celebrity Competence?

One of the severe downsides to celebrity interventions in development politics is oversimplification of issues. The "analysis" rests in the language of rock songs, Hollywood, and [former U.S. president] Ronald Reagan. The world is painted in black and white and good is pitted against evil. Nuance is inevitably lost. Historic experience is disregarded. Celebrities provide their followers with easily understood, morally couched messages, but the process of development is much more complex. As Collier notes, "Inevitably, development buzz has to keep its message simple, driven by the need for slogans, images, and anger. Unfortunately, although the plight of the bottom billion lends itself to simple moralizing, the answers do not."

Therefore, Bono and his fellow celebrity activists might in fact be doing major harm to the peoples of Africa. Their well-meaning interventions probably prolong the tragedy instead of ending it. Rather than raising the ability of Africans to help themselves, celebrity campaigns may well lead the continent into ever deeper trouble. More aid may paralyze the initiative of individuals rather than empowering them. It may even produce a beggar's mentality, where the poor expect the solution to problems from foreign donors rather than from one's own society.

To be sure, Bono does not claim to have expertise in development policy. He is supported by powerful academic economists, in particular Jeffrey Sachs of Columbia University. In fact, Bono and Sachs have become something of a double act, with the professor providing the intellectual message and the rock star bringing it to large audiences. Yet what should one make of Sachs's credentials, especially after his prescriptions of disastrous "shock therapy" for Russia in the transition from communism? [Economist] Jagdish Bhagwati, also at Columbia, has characterized Sachs's intervention in Russia as the biggest debacle of economic policy advice ever.

Now, Sachs advocates another grand strategy, arguing that a Big Push of aid would solve Africa's problems. He estimates that net worldwide foreign aid should reach $195 billion per year in 2015, plus an undisclosed sum for climate change projects. Once again, Sachs advocates the big project and ignores the positive experience that many Asian countries have had with piecemeal reform. His new shock therapy is driven by the old paternalistic attitude that aspires to rescue the world. Sachs appears to be ignoring, willingly or not, that his Big Push is similar to early development policies of the 1950s and 1960s and—to a degree—to the central planning that ruined the countries of Eastern Europe and the USSR [former Soviet Union].

Indeed, why would more aid for Africa—one of the core celebrity urgings, reinforced by Sachs—have positive effects on development when the experience with aid to date has been by and large negative? One of the arguments can be that aid in the past has not achieved the scale required to take the population across the income threshold beyond which the recipients can be on a self-propelled path out of poverty. However, even countries such as Tanzania that did enjoy larger amounts of aid do not provide support for this claim. To continue to ask for more aid flows, despite the failures that are so visible to all who want to see, is surely pushing more good money after bad.

In any case, any further aid must be conditional on improved governance. In the past, development aid frequently supported governments with the worst governance record. Inappropriate governance has clearly been a major obstacle to development in Africa, and improvement of development performance requires new incentive structures that reward success instead of failure. As a recent comprehensive investigation by the Canadian senate concludes, "By far the biggest obstacle to achieving growth and stability in sub-Saharan Africa has been poor government and poor leadership within Africa itself."

The basic components of good governance are well established. The most important ingredients include effective provision of essential public goods and services; law and order; the right to private property; sovereign rights of a country over its mineral and other natural resources; and enforcement of contracts. Yet these elements are missing in many African countries. Markets and private enterprise cannot work in such an institutional vacuum.

Of course, good governance is no panacea for Africa. The intention is not to replace the old aid ideology with yet another simplistic development strategy for Africa. However, providing fresh money, as demanded by celebrity diplomats, ought to be accompanied by proposing clear and plausible strategies for improving governance and by putting in place the necessary institutions and nurturing them to the extent

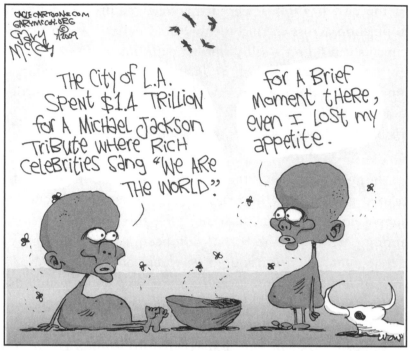

required. Ideally, this improvement of governance should be fostered not in individual states, but in groupings of neighboring countries.

Celebrity Legitimacy?

[Diplomacy and foreign policy expert] Andrew Cooper, in his innovative monograph on celebrity diplomacy, suggests that, unlike other celebrities, Bono has been immunized against criticism. "Because of his imprint as a moral entrepreneur," Cooper argues, "Bono escapes most of the criticism for opportunism and superficial fluff heaped on other celebrities who have taken on a diplomatic profile." Yet there is a case to question the legitimacy of celebrities to speak with authority on development and other international issues.

Celebrities lack a mandate to become active in global politics. People like to listen to the music of Bono and Geldof, but these stars are not democratically elected to public office. Charisma as well as their wallets may give them power, but in most cases celebrities are self-appointed. Their legitimacy is derived from their personal credibility. Thus, one should look more closely at their activities off the campaign trail.

For example, there appears to be a contradiction between Bono's public rhetoric on development and his hard-edged private commercial practices. Bono is a managing director and cofounder of Elevation Partners, which claims to have $1.9 billion in committed capital. In 2006, Elevation Partners became a significant minority shareholder in Forbes Media. Forbes portrays itself as the site for "The World's Business Leaders" and is probably the most conservative publisher in business news.

Bono has also made quite a lot of money from his core business activity. The last tour of U2 consisted of 131 concerts, which resulted in gross ticket receipts of $389 million, the second most successful tour of any rock band in history. The album linked to the tour sold 9 million copies. In contrast to most other bands, U2 owns all rights and sells its merchandise at its concerts.

Of course, Bono can do with his money whatever he likes, but some of his key commercial decisions would appear to sit uncomfortably next to his antipoverty politics. Whereas Bono has chastised politicians for failing adequately to fund antipoverty efforts in Africa, U2 has carefully optimized its own tax bill. In 2006, the band moved part of its corporate base from Ireland to the Netherlands after the Irish government had announced the suspension of tax exemptions that had enabled U2 to collect their songwriting royalties tax-free. Not surprisingly, this shift to the Netherlands, where royalty income remains untaxed, angered quite a few in Bono's native Ireland.

Questions can also be raised concerning the organization of Debt AIDS Trade Africa (DATA), the advocacy association cofounded by Bono in 2002. [DATA and the ONE Campaign merged and became known as ONE in January 2008]. The board of directors of DATA is composed of two women and six men, all of them coming, as Cooper puts it, "from the Anglo-sphere." No board member comes from Africa, and only one of the five DATA offices is located in Africa. Bono does not disclose whether he has donated any of his own funds to the organization.

So, are celebrity diplomats active for the people of Africa or for their own benefit? Cooper argues that "it would be wrong to suggest that the celebrity diplomats from the Anglo-sphere are 'tragedy voyeurs.'" Perhaps, but celebrity diplomats may still use Africa to promote their own agenda, which may or may not be benign. Some citizens actively oppose Bono's work. For example, the so-called GONE project claims to be the "campaign to make Bono history."

More than a Slogan

We have indicated in this [viewpoint] that celebrities are ill-equipped to solve Africa's problems. Rock bands and film stars may help raise awareness of Africa's difficulties, but their campaigns may be counterproductive and could result in an underutilization of African potentials. This is not to advocate a wholesale retreat of outside parties from development efforts in Africa. However, donors have to accept the complexities of development and address them honestly and diligently. The improvement of governance in Africa has to be a core goal, and ownership of development strategies must become much more than a slogan. The alternative would be additional proliferation of celebrity diplomats and a further trivialization of development challenges, the consequences of which are simply too negative to contemplate.

| "The good works these celebrities do are often under the radar."

Celebrities Contribute to Philanthropy

Emily Sweeney

Emily Sweeney is a staff reporter for the Boston Globe. *In the following viewpoint, Sweeney writes that many celebrities participate in philanthropy beyond the glare of the spotlight. She states that recording artists, actors, and television stars in the Boston area donate their time, talent, and resources to local charities and causes. From Oscar-winning actors like Chris Cooper and Geena Davis to music stars like Joe Perry of Aerosmith and JoJo, New England's famous faces do not forget their roots, and they do their part to make life better in their own backyards, Sweeney claims.*

As you read, consider the following questions:

1. According to the author, how did Joe Perry give back to his community?

2. How does Geena Davis support girls' sports, as stated in the viewpoint?

Emily Sweeney, "See the Stars in Your Backyard," *Boston Globe*, September 2, 2007, p. 1. © Copyright 2007 Globe Newspaper Company. Reproduced by permission.

3. What does JoJo tell the author about her hometown?

The stars of music, movies, and television who live in the suburbs south of Boston tend to move about their private lives quietly. So it's not surprising that the good works these celebrities do are often under the radar, too. Yet, despite the lack of Hollywood-like glare, many area celebrities are quietly giving time, talent, and other gifts to make life better in their communities and the world at large.

For example, Duxbury High School alum Juliana Hatfield and Norwood native Dicky Barrett of the Mighty Mighty Bosstones have each donated their musical talent by recording songs for charity albums. The Dropkick Murphys, who started out playing together in the basement of a friend's Quincy barbershop, have played benefit concerts to raise money for My Brother's Keeper, an organization in Easton that delivers food, furniture, and other necessities to needy folks all over southeastern Massachusetts.

Aerosmith guitarist Joe Perry gave two guitars to the Duxbury public schools. He also donated an autographed guitar to a Duxbury Rotary Club auction, where it sold for $12,000 and helped the fire department buy thermal imaging equipment. Perry and his wife, Billie, also worked tirelessly to get the new animal shelter built in Duxbury. The Perrys donated $25,000 to cover the construction costs in 1998, and happily threw the first shovel-full of dirt at the groundbreaking ceremony in December 2004.

In Kingston, Oscar-winning actor Chris Cooper and his wife, Marianne Leone, from the HBO series *The Sopranos*, have been active in town affairs and in advocating for children with special needs. Cooper attended a career day at the local elementary school, and he and his wife have attended school committee meetings. They helped raise money for Handi Kids Summer Camp in Bridgewater, and established the Jesse Cooper Foundation in memory of their 17-year-old son, who died of complications from cerebral palsy in 2005. Jesse was a sophomore at Silver Lake Regional High School. The couple serve on the board of directors of AccesSportAmerica, a non-profit organization that supports athletic programs for people with disabilities.

Jeff Corwin, a Norwell native and host of wildlife television shows on the Animal Planet cable channel, helped launch a new wildlife exhibit at the South Shore Natural Science Center known as the "EcoZone." Corwin, who was named on *People* magazine's 50 Most Beautiful People list, still calls the South Shore home and lives with his wife and daughter in Marshfield.

"Marsh Vegas" is also home to actor Steve Carell, who rose to fame for his role in *The Office* television series. His wife, Cohasset native Nancy Walls, is a former cast member of *Saturday Night Live*. The couple appeared at the Regal Fenway cinema in Boston on June 21 for the premiere of Carell's new comedy, *Evan Almighty*, which was a benefit for the Zachary Carson Brain Tumor Fund, established in honor of a Newton teen who was diagnosed with an inoperable brain tumor in 2005.

Mark Goddard might be best known for his role as Major Don West on the 1960s TV show *Lost in Space*, but his work with children has eclipsed his accomplished acting career. He eventually left show business to go back to school, and earned a master's degree in education from Bridgewater State College. He now works as a special education teacher at the F.L. Chamberlain School in Middleborough, teaching students behavioral management skills, and the occasional improv workshop.

"I've always been involved in working with young people," said Goddard, who lives in Bridgewater with his wife and their 16-year-old son. "It's a wonderful facility, with kids from all over the Northeast," he said. "I work very closely with them."

Goddard said that, in between his acting gigs on the West Coast and on Broadway, he found time to work with children at Head Start programs in California and at the Memorial Sloan-Kettering Cancer Center in New York. He occasionally makes appearances at trade shows to sign autographs for *Lost in Space* buffs, and he still receives fan mail from time to time. He recently began writing a memoir (working title: *To Space and Back*) about his acting career, and his early days growing up in Scituate, including his varsity, basketball days at Scituate High, and teenage pranks that led to run-ins with Weymouth police.

Wareham's own Geena Davis has also been involved with children's advocacy. She graduated from Wareham High School in 1974, and left her hometown to pursue a career in modeling and acting. But she didn't forget her roots. In 1989, the year after she won an Oscar for her performance in *The Accidental Tourist*, she returned to her hometown and led the parade down Main Street during her hometown's 250th anniversary celebration.

Davis is a nationally ranked archer, and a trustee of the Women's Sports Foundation, a charitable educational organization founded by Billie Jean King in 1974. The foundation launched a Web site titled "Geena Takes Aim," (geenatakes aim.com) which provides tools and resources to help promote gender equality in sports.

A message from Davis appears on the front page of the site: "You have the right to play sports and to be the best athlete you can be. But today, your rights may be in jeopardy. Here's what you can do . . ." The site features information about Title IX, online assessment tools to check to see if a particular school is in compliance, and contact information for legislators.

"Did you know that, on the average, 90 percent of all column inches on the sports pages of newspapers goes to men's sports; 5 percent to women's sports, and 3 percent to horse and dog racing? The same is true for television," she said. "Be active in either helping your media celebrate its fair coverage of girls and women in sports, or tweak their habits if they're not getting the job done."

The Women's Sports Foundation recently announced that the Fontbonne Academy Step Squad was awarded a $2,500 grant.

Davis has also embarked on a separate project that addresses the lack of female role models in children's television shows and movies. In 2004 she established See Jane, an organization that is examining gender discrepancy in children's entertainment. Davis raised money to fund research at the University of Southern California that found that there are a disproportionate number of male characters in G-rated movies and TV shows. Davis is working to develop programs to address the imbalance.

Another talented woman from this area, Foxborough's own pop superstar Joanna "JoJo" Levesque, has had a multi-platinum album, a No. 1 hit single on the Billboard charts, an MTV video music award nomination, and roles in major films. The 16-year-old singer has also helped out several charities along the way, including the Tsunami Relief Fund and the Breast Treatment Task Force. She donated her time to record "Come Together Now," a song to benefit the victims of Hurricane Katrina. This month, Levesque will be walking in MetLife's Snoopy in Fashion show during New York's Mercedes-Benz Fashion Week, and after the show the dresses will be auctioned for charity.

Although JoJo spends much of her time on the road touring, she hasn't strayed far from her roots. She said in an interview that she loves "getting my Dunkin' Donut fix when I'm back home" and likes the "realness" of people from around here.

"People are honest. They tell you exactly what they're thinking," she said.

"They're not materialistic. New England, as a whole, is more about family, sports, and barbecues. That's what I like, that kind of camaraderie."

> "Social activism ... is the modern cur-
> rency in Hollywood, forming an impor-
> tant part of a performer's public per-
> sona."

Celebrity Philanthropy
May Not Have an Impact

Gloria Goodale

*In the following viewpoint, Gloria Goodale presents the argu-
ment that celebrity activism is done in part to maintain status
in Hollywood. Public relations professional Richard Laermer believes that a celebrity becomes involved in a cause simply as another business move. Although the author believes that the drive
for good causes comes from a place of self-interest on the part of
Hollywood, celebrities still bring important awareness to needy
places. Gloria Goodale is the Arts and Culture correspondent for
the* Christian Science Monitor.

As you read, consider the following questions:

1. As stated in the viewpoint, what are the two predictable
   events that will occur due to the oil spill in the Gulf of
   Mexico?

Gloria Goodale, "Gulf Oil Spill, Haiti, Darfur: Hollywood Stars Rush to Do Their Bit," *Christian Science Monitor*, June 10, 2010. Reproduced by permisssion.

2. What movie does Richard Laermer suggest is "spot on" in terms of picking a cause in Hollywood?

3. According to the article, who is an exception to the self-interest-driven trend of celebrity activism?

As solutions to the Gulf oil spill elude top experts, at least two events are reassuringly predictable: congressional hearings and the appearance of Hollywood celebrities once the cameras begin to roll.

This week, actor Kevin Costner carted his oil spill cleanup technology up Capitol Hill in hopes of finding an audience for his company (and, say skeptics, his flagging movie career as well).

Take a broader look around the world's hotspots, and the star power increases—director Spike Lee is in Louisiana doing a five-year follow-up to Hurricane Katrina, and Haiti hosted Sean Penn at the same time as George Clooney wrangled Hollywood cohorts into a charity telethon that raised millions.

But as stars seem to be stumbling over themselves to get to the world's neediest regions and biggest causes, the question arises: Has celebrity activism gotten more serious—and meaningful—or is it just bad taste not to have a good cause these days?

The answer is a bit of both, say academics, actors, and PR [public relations] professionals.

"There is more emphasis on the authentic these days," says University of Southern California professor Elizabeth Currid, who has just finished a book on celebrity, called *Starstruck*.

'Social Activism Is the Modern Currency in Hollywood'

Social activism, Ms. Currid points out, is the modern currency in Hollywood, forming an important part of a performer's public persona. Celebrities use it to jockey for position in the entertainment ecosystem. The relationship between celebrities and fans has become less iconic and more accessible, she says, adding that their appeal is more about their personal narrative and less about talent or glamour.

"Activism plays a huge part of that," she says. "And we consume this with an insatiable appetite through new forms of media."

Longtime PR professional, Richard Laermer takes the point further.

"You can't be in Hollywood without a cause these days," he says with a laugh, suggesting that the scene in the film *Bruno* in which star British comedian Sacha Baron Cohen is being tutored on the fine points of a Hollywood career is spot on. Key to it is picking a cause—any cause—he is advised.

Mr. Laermer agrees that more stars are more deeply involved in more issues than ever before. But he says that with few notable exceptions, this is simply another business move.

"Appearing to be socially conscious is the only way to go," he says, adding that whether the commitment is more than skin deep can usually be measured in dollars. "You won't see them touching anything that might actually hurt their careers, and you can bet that Brad Pitt and the rest all have to pay attention to their movie career. If that slumps, you won't see them tromping off to foreign lands quite so quickly."

One of those exceptions—and one whose career took a noticeable hit as a result of his early commitment to weaning western nations from dependence on fossil fuels—is actor Ed Begley, Jr.

Mr. Begley dates his conversion to everything from recycling to electric cars and solar power to Earth Day, 1970.

"It just made so much sense to me," he says, so the performer gave up his car, began using a bicycle and started slowly spreading the word—decades before these actions became politically correct.

Ed Begley's Career Suffered

During the 1990s, he notes, his management pleaded with him, telling him that his career was suffering.

"I didn't believe them until the day in 1992 when I was on a film and they were terrified to tell me that I had to drive a station wagon that wasn't electric," he remembers with a laugh.

"I guess they thought I would just yell at them or something," he says. But he notes that during that entire decade he worked a total of three weeks in US films. He applauds the newfound enthusiasms for social causes in Hollywood.

"These guys who go off to Darfur and India to help people, you have to give them a break for trying to help," he adds.

Professor Currid agrees.

While much of the gusto for good causes may come from self-interest, she notes, celebrities still bring important attention to needy people and places—even though it reflects a culture that consumes these glamorous narratives.

"It's too bad that we seem to need a glamorous star to tell us what we should care about in our personal lives," she says.

Periodical Bibliography

The following articles have been selected to supplement the diverse views presented in this chapter.

Dennis AuBuchon   "Celebrity Endorsements and Their Impact," *American Chronicle*, October 27, 2008.

Saabira Chaudhuri   "Hollywood's Most Influential Celebrity Activists," *Forbes*, November 22, 2006.

Douglas A. Hicks   "The Limits of Celebrity Activism," *Christian Century*, March 21, 2006.

Lynn Hirschberg   "M.I.A.'s Agitprop Pop," *New York Times*, May 25, 2010.

Asteris Huliaras   "Celebrity Activism in International Relations: In Search of a Framework for Analysis," *Global Society*, April 2010.

Tom Junod   "Angelina Jolie Dies for Our Sins," *Esquire*, July 1, 2007.

Peter Knegt   "The Collision of Politics, Celebrity and the Media: Barry Levinson Goes to 'PoliWood,'" indieWIRE, April 24, 2009. www.indiewire.com.

Tolu Olorunda   "Bono Bombs, Again: Celebrity Politics & Why the Music Industry Is No Victim," AllHipHop.com, January 11, 2010. http://allhiphop.com.

Maria Puente   "Hail to the Chief Celebrity? That's Politics Mixed with Entertainment," *USA Today*, October 12, 2008.

Nathalie Rothschild   "Mia Farrow: Dieting for the Cause," *Spiked*, May 14, 2009. www.spiked-online.com.

OPPOSING
VIEWPOINTS®
SERIES

CHAPTER 4

What Is the Future of Celebrity Culture?

Chapter Preface

Named after the entertainment industry's thirty-mile zone around the Los Angeles intersection of West Beverly and La Cienega boulevards, TMZ.com became a major force in celebrity news since its launch in 2005. TMZ was the first to report music icon Michael Jackson's death in June 2009, hotel heiress Paris Hilton's forty-five-day jail sentence in May 2007, and singer Britney Spears's petition for divorce from her husband, Kevin Federline, in November 2006. "We are totally wired in this town,"[1] says editor in chief Harvey Levin. "[T]here's still this residual but not yet vestigial instinct to think 'Oh, it's just TMZ, let's wait for the Associated Press or the *New York Times* or the *Los Angeles Times* before we can say it's true.' . . . I don't think in, say, five years, that will be the case."

TMZ, nonetheless, does not escape criticism or misjudgments in its quest to break Hollywood headlines before any other source. In February 2009, the site released a police photo of Rihanna, taken after her then boyfriend and fellow recording artist, Chris Brown, had beaten her—while it was still being treated as evidence. In December that year, TMZ published a doctored image of John F. Kennedy surrounded by nude women on a ship, claiming it was authentic. In addition, critics charge that TMZ paparazzi invasively pursue celebrities and that the site contains lurid, sensational content. In the *Cornell Daily Sun*, Tony Manfred writes that "it can show all the borderline pornographic clips that *Entertainment Tonight* and *Access Hollywood* can't."[2] Amid such allegations, Levin defends TMZ and how it gets the story, including signed agreements that its photographers do not flout the law. "We have

1. New York Times, June 26, 2009. www.nytimes.com.
2. *Cornell Daily Sun*, September 17, 2007. http://cornellsun.com.

real boundaries,"[3] he says. In the following chapter, the authors discuss how the celebrity culture is changing in the twenty-first century.

3. *Toronto Sun*, May 12, 2009. www.torontosun.com.

> *"So pervasive has celebrity become in contemporary American life that one now begins to hear a good deal about a phenomenon known as the Culture of Celebrity."*

Celebrity Culture Is Pervasive

Joseph Epstein

Joseph Epstein is a contributing editor to the Weekly Standard *and author of several books including* Snobbery: The American Version *and* Friendship: An Exposé. *In the following viewpoint, Epstein claims that the culture of celebrity has invaded every sphere of American life. He proposes that "celebrity-creating machinery" is at work: Television shows, magazines, newspapers, and blogs turn individuals with little achievement or talent into famous faces. In this culture, Epstein asserts that publicity—good and bad—is of highest value, measured in newspaper inches and airtime. As for the stars, they fulfill the public's need to witness spectacular triumph and failure to place their lives into context, he concludes.*

As you read, consider the following questions:

1. To Epstein, what is the distinction between celebrity and fame?

2. How does the author characterize modern celebrity?

3. According to Epstein, what is behind the categorization of celebrities?

Celebrity at this moment in America is epidemic, and it's spreading fast, sometimes seeming as if nearly everyone has got it. Television provides celebrity dance contests, celebrities take part in reality shows, perfumes carry the names not merely of designers but of actors and singers. Without celebrities, whole sections of the *New York Times* and the *Washington Post* would have to close down. So pervasive has celebrity become in contemporary American life that one now begins to hear a good deal about a phenomenon known as the Culture of Celebrity.

The word "culture" no longer, I suspect, stands in most people's minds for that whole congeries of institutions, relations, kinship patterns, linguistic forms, and the rest for which the early anthropologists meant it to stand. Words, unlike disciplined soldiers, refuse to remain in place and take orders. They insist on being unruly, and slither and slide around, picking up all sorts of slippery and even goofy meanings. An icon, as we shall see, doesn't stay a small picture of a religious personage but usually turns out nowadays to be someone with spectacular grosses. "The language," as [French writer Gustave] Flaubert once protested in his attempt to tell his mistress Louise Colet how much he loved her, "is inept."

Today, when people glibly refer to "the corporate culture," "the culture of poverty," "the culture of journalism," "the culture of the intelligence community"—and "community" has, of course, itself become another of those hopelessly baggy-pants words, so that one hears talk even of "the homeless community"—what I think is meant by "culture" is the general emotional atmosphere and institutional character surrounding the word to which "culture" is attached. Thus, corporate culture is thought to breed selfishness practiced at the Machiavellian [referring to Niccolò Machiavelli's principles marked by duplicity] level; the culture of poverty, hopelessness and despair; the culture of journalism, a taste for the sensational combined with a short attention span; the culture of the intelligence community, covering-one's-own-behind viperishness; and so on. Culture used in this way is also brought in to explain unpleasant or at least dreary behavior. "The culture of NASA [National Aeronautics and Space Administration] has to be changed," is a sample of its current usage. The comedian Flip Wilson, after saying something outrageous, would revert to the refrain line, "The debbil made me do it." So, today, when admitting to unethical or otherwise wretched behavior, people often say, "The culture made me do it."

As for "celebrity," the standard definition is no longer the dictionary one but rather closer to the one that Daniel Boorstin gave in his book *The Image: Or What Happened to the American Dream*: "The celebrity," Boorstin wrote, "is a person who is well-known for his well-knownness," which is improved in its frequently misquoted form as "a celebrity is someone famous for being famous." The other standard quotation on this subject is [artist] Andy Warhol's "In the future everyone will be world-famous for fifteen minutes," which also frequently turns up in an improved misquotation as "everyone will have his fifteen minutes of fame."

But to say that a celebrity is someone well-known for being well-known, though clever enough, doesn't quite cover it. Not that there is a shortage of such people who seem to be known only for their well-knownness. What do a couple named Sid and Mercedes Bass do, except appear in boldface in the *New York Times* "Sunday Styles" section and other such venues (as we now call them) of equally shimmering insignificance, often standing next to Ahmet and Mica Ertegun, also well-known for being well-known? Many moons ago, journalists used to refer to royalty as "face cards"; today celebrities are perhaps best thought of as bold faces, for as such do their names often appear in the press (and in a *New York Times* column with that very name, Bold Face).

The distinction between celebrity and fame is one most dictionaries tend to fudge. I suspect everyone has, or prefers to make, his own. The one I like derives not from Aristotle, who didn't have to trouble with celebrities, but from the career of [baseball player] Ted Williams. A sportswriter once said that he, Williams, wished to be famous but had no interest in being a celebrity. What Ted Williams wanted to be famous for was his hitting. He wanted everyone who cared about baseball to know that he was—as he believed and may well have been—the greatest pure hitter who ever lived. What he didn't want to do was to take on any of the effort off the baseball field involved in making this known. As an active player, Williams gave no interviews, signed no baseballs or photographs, chose not to be obliging in any way to journalists or fans. A rebarbative character, not to mention often a slightly menacing s.o.b., Williams, if you had asked him, would have said that it was enough that he was the last man to hit .400; he did it on the field, and therefore didn't have to sell himself off the field. As for his duty to his fans, he didn't see that he had any.

Whether Ted Williams was right or wrong to feel as he did is of less interest than the distinction his example provides, which suggests that fame is something one earns—through talent or achievement of one kind or another—while celebrity is something one cultivates or, possibly, has thrust upon one. The two are not, of course, entirely exclusive. One can be immensely talented and full of achievement and yet wish to broadcast one's fame further through the careful cultivation of celebrity; and one can have the thinnest of achievements and be talentless and yet be made to seem otherwise through the mechanics and dynamics of celebrity-creation, in our day a whole mini-(or maybe not so mini) industry of its own.

Or, another possibility, one can become a celebrity with scarcely any pretense to talent or achievement whatsoever. Much modern celebrity seems the result of careful promotion or great good luck or something besides talent and achievement: Mr. Donald Trump, Ms. Paris Hilton, Mr. Regis Philbin, take a bow. The ultimate celebrity of our time may have been John F. Kennedy Jr., notable only for being his parents' very handsome son—both his birth and good looks factors beyond his control—and, alas, known for nothing else whatsoever now, except for the sad, dying-young-Adonis end to his life.

Fame, then, at least as I prefer to think of it, is based on true achievement; celebrity on the broadcasting of that achievement, or the inventing of something that, if not scrutinized too closely, might pass for achievement. Celebrity suggests ephemerality, while fame has a chance of lasting, a shot at reaching the happy shores of posterity.

Oliver Goldsmith, in his poem "The Deserted Village," refers to "good fame," which implies that there is also a bad or false fame. Bad fame is sometimes thought to be fame in the present, or fame on earth, while good fame is that bestowed by posterity—those happy shores again. (Which doesn't eliminate the desire of most of us, at least nowadays, to have our fame here and hereafter, too.) Not false but wretched fame is covered by the word "infamy"—"Infamy, infamy, infamy," remarked the English wit Frank Muir, "they all have it in for me"—while the lower, or pejorative, order of celebrity is covered by the word "notoriety," also frequently misused to mean noteworthiness.

Leo Braudy's magnificent book on the history of fame, *The Frenzy of Renown*, illustrates how the means of broadcasting fame have changed over the centuries: from having one's head engraved on coins, to purchasing statuary of oneself, to (for the really high rollers—Alexander the Great, the Caesar boys) naming cities or even months after oneself, to commissioning painted portraits, to writing books or having books written about one, and so on into our day of the publicity or press agent, the media blitz, the public relations expert, and the egomaniacal blogger. One of the most successful of public-relations experts, Ben Sonnenberg Sr., used to say that he saw it as his job to construct very high pedestals for very small men.

Which leads one to a very proper suspicion of celebrity. As [author] George Orwell said about saints, so it seems only sensible to say about celebrities: They should all be judged guilty until proven innocent. Guilty of what, precisely? I'd say of the fraudulence (however minor) of inflating their brilliance, accomplishments, worth, of passing themselves off as something they aren't, or at least are not quite. If fraudulence is the crime, publicity is the means by which the caper is brought off.

The Values of Celebrity

Is the current heightened interest in the celebrated sufficient to form a culture—a culture of a kind worthy of study? The anthropologist Alfred Kroeber defined culture, in part, as embodying "values which may be formulated (overtly as mores) or felt (implicitly as in folkways) by the society carrying the culture, and which it is part of the business of the anthropologist to characterize and define." What are the values of celebrity culture? They are the values, almost exclusively, of publicity. Did they spell one's name right? What was the size and composition of the audience? Did you check the receipts? Was the timing right? Publicity is concerned solely with effects and does not investigate causes or intrinsic value too closely. For example, a few years ago a book of mine called *Snobbery: The American Version* received what I thought was a too greatly mixed review in the *New York Times Book Review*. I remarked on my disappointment to the publicity man at my publisher's, who promptly told me not to worry: It was a full-page review, on page 11, right-hand side. That, he said, "is very good real estate," which was quite as important as, perhaps more important than, the reviewer's actual words and final judgment. Better to be tepidly considered on page 11 than extravagantly praised on page 27, left-hand side. Real estate, man, it's the name of the game.

We must have new names, [author] Marcel Proust presciently noted—in fashion, in medicine, in art, there must always be new names. It's a very smart remark, and the fields Proust chose seem smart, too, at least for his time. (Now there must also be new names, at a minimum, among movie stars and athletes and politicians.) Implicit in Proust's remark is the notion that if the names don't really exist, if the quality isn't there to sustain them, it doesn't matter; new names we shall have in any case. And every sophisticated society somehow, more or less implicitly, contrives to supply them.

I happen to think that we haven't had a major poet writing in English since perhaps the death of W.H. Auden or, to lower the bar a little, Philip Larkin. But new names are put forth nevertheless—high among them in recent years has been that of Seamus Heaney—because, after all, what kind of a time could we be living in if we didn't have a major poet? And besides there are all those prizes that, year after year, must be given out, even if so many of the recipients don't seem quite worthy of them.

Considered as a culture, celebrity does have its institutions. We now have an elaborate celebrity-creating machinery well in place—all those short-attention-span television shows (*Entertainment Tonight*, *Access Hollywood*, *Lifestyles of the Rich and Famous*); all those magazines (beginning with *People* and far from ending with the *National Enquirer*). We have high-priced celebrity-mongers—[talk show hosts] Barbara Walters, Diane Sawyer, Jay Leno, David Letterman, Oprah—who not

"Homeless in Hollywood," cartoon by Henrik Rehr. www.CartoonStock.com.

only live off others' celebrity but also, through their publicity-making power, confer it and have in time become very considerable celebrities each in his or her own right.

Without the taste for celebrity, they would have to close down the whole Style section of every newspaper in the country. Then there is the celebrity profile (in *Vanity Fair, Esquire, Gentlemen's Quarterly*; these are nowadays usually orchestrated by a press agent, with all touchy questions declared out-of-bounds), or the television talk-show interview with a star, which is beyond parody. Well, almost beyond: [comedian] Martin Short in his parody of a talk-show host remarked to the actor Kiefer Sutherland, "You're Canadian, aren't you? What's that all about?"

Yet we still seem never to have enough celebrities, so we drag in so-called "It Girls" (Paris Hilton, Cindy Crawford, other supermodels), tired television hacks (Regis Philbin, Ed McMahon), back-achingly boring but somehow sacrosanct news anchors (Walter Cronkite, Tom Brokaw). Toss in what I think of as the lower-class punditi, who await calls from various television news and chat shows to demonstrate their locked-in political views and meager expertise on major and cable stations alike: Pat Buchanan, Eleanor Clift, Mark Shields, Robert Novak, Michael Beschloss, and the rest. Ah, if only [comedian] Lenny Bruce were alive today, he could do a scorchingly cruel bit about [psychologist] Dr. Joyce Brothers sitting by the phone wondering why [tabloid talk show host] Jerry Springer never calls.

Floating upon "Hype"

Many of our current-day celebrities float upon "hype," which is really a publicist's gas used to pump up and set aloft something that doesn't really quite exist. Hype has also given us a new breakdown, or hierarchical categorization, of celebrities. Until twenty-five or so years ago great celebrities were called "stars," a term first used in the movies and entertainment and then taken up by sports, politics, and other fields. Stars proving a bit drab, "superstars" were called in to play, this term beginning in sports but fairly quickly branching outward. Apparently too many superstars were about, so the trope was switched from astronomy to religion, and we now have "icons." All this takes Proust's original observation a step further: the need for new names to call the new names.

This new ranking—stars, superstars, icons—helps us believe that we live in interesting times. One of the things celebrities do for us is suggest that in their lives they are fulfilling our fantasies. Modern celebrities, along with their fame, tend to be wealthy or, if not themselves beautiful, able to acquire beautiful lovers. Their celebrity makes them, in the view of many, worthy of worship. "So long as man remains free," [Russian author Fyodor] Dostoevsky writes in the Grand Inquisitor section of *The Brothers Karamazov*, "he strives for nothing so incessantly and painfully as to find someone to worship." If contemporary celebrities are the best thing on offer as living gods for us to worship, this is not good news.

But the worshipping of celebrities by the public tends to be thin, and not uncommonly it is nicely mixed with loathing. We also, after all, at least partially, like to see our celebrities as frail, ready at all times to crash and burn. [Actor] Cary Grant once warned the then-young director Peter Bogdanovich, who was at the time living with [actress] Cybill Shepherd, to stop telling people he was in love. "And above all," Grant warned, "stop telling them you're happy." When Bogdanovich asked why, Cary Grant answered, "Because they're not in love and they're not happy. . . . Just remember, Peter, people do not like beautiful people."

Grant's assertion is borne out by our grocery press, the *National Enquirer*, the *Star*, the *Globe*, and other variants of the English gutter press. All these tabloids could as easily travel under the generic title of the National Schadenfreude [German word meaning enjoyment resulting from others' misfortune], for more than half the stories they contain come under the category of "See How the Mighty Have Fallen": Oh, my, I see where that bright young television sitcom star, on a drug binge again, had to be taken to a hospital in an ambulance! To think that the handsome movie star has been cheating on his wife all these years—snakes loose in the Garden of Eden, evidently! Did you note that the powerful senator's drinking has caused him to embarrass himself yet again in public? I see where that immensely successful Hollywood couple turns out to have had a child who died of anorexia! Who'd've thought?

How pleasing to learn that our own simpler, less moneyed, unglamorous lives are, in the end, much to be preferred to those of these beautiful, rich, and powerful people, whose vast publicity has diverted us for so long and whose fall proves even more diverting now. "As would become a lifelong habit for most of us," Thomas McGuane writes in a recent short story in the *New Yorker* called "Ice," "we longed to witness spectacular achievement and modifying failure. Neither of these things, we were discreetly certain, would ever come to us; we would instead be granted the frictionless lives of the meek."

Publicity Bores

Along with trying to avoid falling victim to schadenfreude, celebrities, if they are clever, do well to regulate the amount of publicity they allow to cluster around them. And not celebrities alone. Edith Wharton, having published too many stories and essays in a great single rush in various magazines during a concentrated period, feared, as she put it, the danger of becoming "a magazine bore." Celebrities, in the same way, are in danger of becoming publicity bores, though few among them seem to sense it. Because of improperly rationed publicity, along with a substantial helping of self-importance, the comedian Bill Cosby will never again be funny. The actress Elizabeth McGovern said of Sean Penn that he "is brilliant, brilliant at being the kind of reluctant celebrity." At the level of high culture, Saul Bellow used to work this bit quite well on the literary front, making every interview (and there have been hundreds of them) feel as if given only with the greatest reluctance, if not under actual duress. Others are brilliant at regulating their publicity. [Talk show host] Johnny Carson was very intelligent about carefully husbanding his celebrity, choosing not to come out of retirement, except at exactly the right time or when the perfect occasion presented itself. Apparently it never did. Given the universally generous obituary tributes he received, dying now looks, for him, to have been an excellent career move.

Careful readers will have noticed that I referred above to "the actress Elizabeth McGovern" and felt no need to write anything before or after the name Sean Penn. True celebrities need nothing said of them in apposition, fore or aft. The greatest celebrities are those who don't even require their full names mentioned: Marilyn, Johnny, Liz, Liza, Oprah, Michael (could be Jordan or Jackson—context usually clears this up fairly quickly), Kobe, Martha (Stewart, not Washington), Britney, Shaq, J.Lo, Frank (Sinatra, not Perdue), O.J., and, with the quickest recognition and shortest name of all—trumpets here, please—W.

One has the impression that being a celebrity was easier at any earlier time than it is now, when celebrity-creating institutions, from paparazzi to gutter-press exposés to television talk-shows, weren't as intense, as full-court press, as they are today. In the *Times Literary Supplement*, a reviewer of a biography of Margot Fonteyn noted that Miss Fonteyn "was a star from a more respectful age of celebrity, when keeping one's distance was still possible." My own candidate for the perfect celebrity in the twentieth century would be Noël Coward, a man in whom talent combined with elegance to give off the glow of glamour—and also a man who would have known how to fend off anyone wishing to investigate his private life. Today, instead of elegant celebrities, we have celebrity criminal trials: Michael Jackson, Kobe Bryant, Martha Stewart, Robert Blake, Winona Ryder, and O.J. Simpson. Schadenfreude is in the saddle again.

American society in the twenty-first century, received opinion has it, values only two things: money and celebrity. Whether or not this is true, vast quantities of money, we know, will buy celebrity. The very rich—John D. Rockefeller and powerful people of his era—used to pay press agents to keep their names out of the papers. But today one of the things money buys is a place at the table beside the celebrated, with the celebrities generally delighted to accommodate, there to share some of the glaring light. An example is Mort Zuckerman, who made an early fortune in real estate, has bought magazines and newspapers, and is now himself among the punditi, offering his largely unexceptional political views on *The McLaughlin Group* and other television chat shows. Which is merely another way of saying that, whether or not celebrity in and of itself constitutes a culture, it has certainly penetrated and permeated much of American culture generally.

| "After 30 years, this cycle of American
celebrity mania has peaked."

Celebrity Culture Is Fading

Kurt Andersen

In the following viewpoint, Kurt Andersen contends that the culture of celebrity is reaching its peak in America. The critical mass of magazines, gossip columns, and television shows, Andersen maintains, has turned celebrities into figures the public knows on a seemingly intimate and mundane basis, the dull details of stars' lives deemed newsworthy. According to the author, this media saturation has resulted in a marked decline in ratings of entertainment programs and newsstand sales of tabloids, revealing that society's fascination with celebrity ebbs and flows. Andersen is a writer, novelist, and former editor in chief of New York Magazine.

As you read, consider the following questions:

1. How were celebrity tabloids transformed in 1974, in Andersen's view?

2. How did *Us Weekly* demystify stars, according to Andersen?

3. How does the author back his claim that celebrity publications and shows are declining?

On a scale of one to ten, one being the least possible interest in famous entertainers qua famous entertainers, and ten being the most, I'm about a six. Until I recently gorged for days on end, it had been years since I had touched a copy of *People* or *Us Weekly*. I skipped the Tonys and Grammys and Emmys. But I do skim three or four New York newspaper gossip columns most weekdays, and I watched E!'s Golden Globes red-carpet preshow, and, of course, I tuned in to the Academy Awards telecast. For years, I've thought that the intense fascination with famous people must be about to end—and I've been repeatedly, egregiously mistaken. But now—truly, finally—I believe that we are at the apogee, the zenith, the plateau, the top of the market. After 30 years, this cycle of American celebrity mania has peaked. I think. I hope.

Of course, at the newsstand and on TV, the unprecedented frenzy seems to be proceeding apace. The dozen women appearing on the big women's magazines in any recent month (Lindsay Lohan, Hilary Duff, Madonna, Keira Knightley, Ashlee Simpson, Sarah Jessica Parker, Kate Beckinsale, Natalie Portman, etcetera) will be pretty much the same ones next month, unless Jennifer Aniston or Angelina Jolie deigns to make herself available.

Magazine editors gripe about the rings they have to jump through to book the hottest possible celebrities ("The PR people," one complained to me, "are really such f---ing f--- brains"), but they still do whatever's necessary. And the jonesing for any speck of celebrity pixie dust can have a crackwhore quality. An editor of one upscale magazine was genuinely thrilled last year that she had persuaded Julie Delpy to pose for her cover. "Who is Julie Delpy?" I asked. The editor and I each considered the other deeply, tragically out of it.

The increasing celebrotropism of general-interest magazines and news shows, though, has been a steady, gradual thing. But what's new is the critical mass of highly visible media devoted to enabling the celebrity-besotted Everyperson's fantasy that she is intimately acquainted with celebrities (*People, In Touch, Access, ET*)—no, even more intimate (*Newlyweds: Nick and Jessica*, VH1's "Celebreality" shows); that she's really no different from the celebrities (*Us, Star*); that as the virtual pal of the renowed it's only natural that she know which brand of seltzer and skin cleanser and earrings and panties they buy (*In Style, Life & Style, Celebrity Living*), so that she can purchase the very same ones for herself; and that an ordinary schmo like her might actually be embraced by the quasi-famous (*Dancing with the Stars, Skating with Celebrities*) or even become famous herself (*American Idol*).

We don't yet have the technology to create a collective fantasy realm with the seamless verisimilitude of *The Matrix*, but this is another large beta step in that direction. Today as never before, tens of millions of American women inhabit Celebrity World. "My generation," says *Us Weekly* editor Janice Min, who's 35, "thinks of celebrities as their peers—like neighbors, or people you went to high school with. They're on a first-name basis with them." And for her generation, an iconic movie was *Single White Female*, in which Jennifer Jason Leigh's nutty character appropriates Bridget Fonda's clothes and look and life.

How did it come to this? As recently as the seventies, magazines all about celebrities were beneath contempt for respectable people, a small, nearly invisible media ghetto—or, rather, media trailer park. One bought a copy of the *National Enquirer* (ELVIS TO MARRY CHER!) only as a bit of jokey slumming. The movie-star magazines that had been born with Hollywood—the *Modern Screens* and the *Photoplays*—were fading away. In the age of Vietnam and rock and roll and revolution, they seemed preposterously cheesy and irrelevant.

Then came the new zero year, 1974. The *Enquirer* went legit, the *National Star* was launched, and Time Inc. created

People. Us and *Entertainment Tonight* followed soon after. The national hunger was not slaked, however, but turned into a 24/7 binge. In 1999, there was just one glossy celebrity weekly. Now there are seven. As the rest of print hunkers down, resisting or resigning itself to the end of a media century, it seems as if the only new publications are about celebrities, like an algae bloom—chartreuse scum!—suddenly covering the surface of an old, sick pond.

In some ways, the weeklies are all alike. In the glossies, everyone but superstars (Oprah, Howard Stern) disappears after 50, so given the enormous maw that must be fed, celebrity has been defined down. Ellen Pompeo? Joshua Jackson? Stacy Keibler, a pro wrestler and one of the "stars" on *Dancing with the Stars*, was the subject of lifestyle features in two magazines the same week. And if those people count as celebrities, then the most banal details of the lives of actual stars count as news. Sharon Stone shopped at a flooring store. Luke Wilson parked at a meter on the street. Jennifer Aniston and Vince Vaughn did not attend a comedy show in Las Vegas. Astonishingly, each of those dull, mingy bits of color were enough to justify a stand-alone item.

But each weekly also has its special flavor, which can be plotted along two axes—meanness and class. *People* is far and away the classiest and least mean, as well as the most old-school. In addition to coverage of Brad and Angelina, *People* runs pieces about Dick Cheney, the Alabama church fires, and Texas prison mothers.

Us Weekly was successfully reinvented four years ago as the flashier, shallower, bitchier kid sister to *People. In Touch*, on the other braid, passingly refers to Jennifer Garner as "ultrafit" and Ben Affleck as "buffer than ever." The *Star's* friendliness is more corporate: No other magazine runs as many purely promotional pictures and items about new movies and TV shows. The Brits behind the new Americanized *OK!* call what they do "relationship journalism," which means 100 percent fulsomeness in the old mid-century fashion: "Angelina Opens Her Heart to *OK!*"

But none of the magazines (as opposed to the tabloids) seems gratuitously mean about stars except in the interest of reassuring the reader that celebrities are almost as flawed and ordinary as she is. In the *Us Weekly* photo section called "Stars—They're Just Like *Us!*" every headline repeats the mantra as a kind of retard haiku: "They buy groceries!" (Anna Kournikova) and "They bite into hoagies!" (Nicole Richie). *Star* ran a startling pair of full-page photos of Calista Flockhart ungroomed and, six hours later, impeccably glamorized—and speculated about the specific L'Oréal and Maybelline products that may have transmuted Calista from an exhausted, scowling slug-like-them to a dazzling, girlish hottie.

This is postmodern democracy. The stars are brought down to the plebeians' level—but now the plebes are also provided with exhaustive instructions for achieving the hallucination that they are just like the stars. *In Style* pioneered the back half of the equation, and still executes its upper-middlebrow, Uma-Gwyneth-Prada version impeccably. (Although I have a question: Did a Time Inc. fact-checker *really* confirm that Demi Moore wears a blue La Mystère embroidered-Swiss-tulle-lace bra?)

Dozens of pages of simulate-a-celebrity-lifestyle guides now appear in the magazines at every caste stratum. The same week *Celebrity Living* informed readers that celebrities were into skull motifs, *Star* was on the case, too: "Stars are boning up on fashion's latest trend: skulls! They're adding a cool edge to everything from cashmere tops to belts and bags." You can suck the candy sucked by Mary-Kate Olsen. You can even buy the same battery charger the stars use.

Would you like to receive messages from (okay, about) your imaginary friends? *People* offers instant wireless "celebrity updates." Enter the Matrix; embrace the fantasy. Accord-

The Waning of Celebrity Journalism

What the hell has happened to our national gossip business?

In the past decade, the rag trade had exploded, bringing vaguely shameful joy to millions of transatlantic travelers, subway commuters, grocery store shoppers and those languishing in doctors' offices. But now it seems a confluence of events has changed the manner in which America gobbles its vapid information about celebrities. The pleasure we take in snurfling through the trash bins of those more rich and famous than we seems to be waning, leaving me a little sad—bereft of mindless reading material when hanging out in major transportation hubs—but perhaps, at the end of the day, just a little less dumb.

Rebecca Traister,
"Who the Hell Are Heidi and Spencer?"
Salon, *March 20, 2008. www.salon.com.*

ing to the *Times,* fashionable young women in cities like New York have now started wearing warm-weather clothes during the winter because they are unconsciously driven by ubiquitous "images of demiclad stars pushing strollers and sipping lattes" on "E! Entertainment and [in] celebrity magazines"—to make-believe they're in Brentwood or Malibu.

It has gotten slightly insane. And I don't mean figuratively.

But as I said at the outset, I have a hunch that the glut has finally reached a saturation point. The fever may be breaking.

The Nielsen ratings for this year's Oscars were down 8 percent, and for the Grammys 11 percent. During the last half of 2005, the *Enquirer*'s newsstand sales were down by a quarter and *Entertainment Weekly*'s by 30 percent. The American

OK! is said to be unwell, the magazine *Inside TV* was launched and killed last year, and a magazine called *Star Shop* was killed before it launched.

Like other American social tides, the fascination with celebrities has been cyclical, and after several decades of rising (as it also did front the twenties through the forties), perhaps it will now (as in the sixties) ebb. However, one difference this time is the fractured nature of mass culture: Because Americans no longer all watch the same TV shows and listen to the same music, they may feel a more desperate need to immerse themselves in the private lives of a few, almost arbitrary pseudo-superstars (*Jessica Simpson?*)—to feel the glamour by stalking the performers, since the performances don't matter so much anymore.

But the designated media gatekeepers are saying that Paris Hilton, the very embodiment of modern celebrity black magic, is over. Maybe she's the canary in the mine, whose end heralds the end of this extreme era. At the dénouement of our last celebrity-media-mad epoch, in the *Sweet Smell of Success* fifties, there was another sexy, slutty young Hilton whom the gossip rags obsessed over. Nicky Hilton, the great-uncle of Paris (and namesake of her sister), dated Mamie Van Doren, Natalie Wood, and Joan Collins, and married Elizabeth Taylor. By the time he died druggily in 1969, however, the public couldn't have cared less, and the celebrity media that had made him briefly famous were dead or dying as well. So perhaps we won't always have Paris.

> "A new kind of fame . . . is changing our celebrity culture, a fame that is increasingly disconnected from the star's success in the field for which he or she is ostensibly famous."

Many Celebrities Are Famous for Being Famous

Amy Argetsinger

Amy Argetsinger is a staff writer for the Washington Post's *Style section. In the following viewpoint, Argetsinger offers a new category of celebrity—"famesque"—wherein the star is primarily famous for his or her fame. For instance, she claims that British actress Sienna Miller is better known for her personal life, fashion choices, and interview flubs than her film career or talents. As entertainment news became a round-the-clock industry, the exploits of Miller, Jessica Simpson, and others began to fill the void of celebrity news, Argetsinger says. The author insists that famesque stars maintain the momentum of press with their provocative behavior and skilled publicists.*

As you read, consider the following questions:

1. According to the author, how is "famesque" different from other types of celebrity?

2. How did Miller gain fame, in the author's view?

3. What traits do the famesque share, as stated by Argetsinger?

For five years, we've followed the golden girl. Sienna Miller smiles from magazine covers. She dominates the red carpets. She's a regular on TMZ.

And she's suffered, so prettily, the burden of her fame: The humiliating breakups laid bare in the press. The blowback from careless interviews. The "homewrecker" catcalls in the blogosphere. The shame of topless photos, caught on vacation, now all over the tabs; all the horrible invasions of privacy.

Right about now you're thinking, "Who's Sienna Miller again? Remind me why I'm supposed to know her?"

It's okay! There's absolutely no reason you should know who she is—not even if you're a religious follower of the celebrity press that tracks her so closely. She's an actress, but odds are you've never seen a single one of her movies or TV shows. Miller is a pioneer in a new kind of fame that is changing our celebrity culture, a fame that is increasingly disconnected from the star's success in the field for which he or she is ostensibly famous.

Sienna Miller is not famous. She is *famesque.*

What is famesque? It's not the paradox of the unlovable A-lister—the Nicole Kidman types who win all the awards but lose the hearts of the multiplex. It's not the quandary of the shrinking star (Ricky Martin), gossip-bait still on the strength of a few decade-old monster hits. The famesque are distinct from their has-been cousins who extended their run via reality shows and basic-cable hosting gigs (Bill Rancic, Mario

Lopez) and from the train wrecks (Lindsay Lohan) whose detour from genuine fame is compelling because they had it and blew it.

The famesque of 2009 are descended from that dawn-of-TV creation, the Famous for Being Famous. Turn on a talk show or *Hollywood Squares* and there'd be Zsa Zsa Gabor, Dr. Joyce Brothers, Charles Nelson Reilly, so friendly and familiar and—what was it they did again? But the FFBF always seemed to know how marginal they were—that was their charm. And they never, ever made the cover of *People*.

The truly famesque possess the seeming gravitas that comes with a title and the suggestion of a job—actor, singer, pro athlete. It's just that . . . you've never seen them act, or heard them sing, or watched them play. Instead: You read about them. A lot. There was a time when the growth of our worldwide round-the-clock entertainment-news industry was gravely threatened by the fact that there weren't enough legitimate celebrities to power it—until the famesque stepped in to fill that market niche. They single-handedly saved TMZ's business model. Because, hey, it's not every day Mel Gibson gets drunk and insults a cop.

So: Sienna Miller, the most famous obscure art house film star in history. The celebrity press often drops the name of a star's most recent or biggest project to remind you who they are. For Miller, it's *Factory Girl* (2006), in which she starred as drug-damaged '60s scenester Edie Sedgwick. You remember—the one you read about, where she got the role after Katie Holmes suddenly dropped out. But you didn't see it, right? It made only $1.6 million in U.S. theaters. Miller's biggest-grossing movie was a fantasy-adventure called *Stardust*, in which she was billed about sixth or seventh behind Michelle Pfeiffer and Robert De Niro. Not that you saw that one either: It made only $39 million, not a lot for that kind of thing.

Then how'd she become so famesque? *Us Weekly* News Director Lara Cohen, who says she's been with the magazine "since the era of Bennifer One," says it started with being incredibly photogenic. At the time, maybe five years ago, Miller had one big hit film in the UK (*Layer Cake*, which never took off here) and a lot of buzz. "A lot of the photo agencies we work with are based in London," Cohen said. "So we were seeing a lot of photos of her. But she was interesting as a style icon in a way that Jordan or some of the other British celebrities were not." (We don't know who Jordan is either.)

Miller gained momentum, Cohen says, with her knack for "no-holds-barred, watch-your-mouth interviews." As during the filming of *The Mysteries of Pittsburgh*, when Miller, interviewed by *Rolling Stone*, slammed her host city as "[rhymes-with-Pitts]burgh." Says Cohen: "It was the most publicity that movie got." (It grossed less than $100,000.)

And Miller harnessed the power of celebrity dating, where "one plus one equals four," Cohen says. Take Posh Spice, whose union with soccer star David Beckham catapulted her to heights poor Sporty and Scary could never climb. It's the reason *Us* last month gave the breaking-news treatment to the divorce of Eddie Cibrian. Who? Some guy who used to be on *Third Watch*, apparently—but word is he was maybe dating LeAnn Rimes. Miller became famesque by dating Jude Law . . . and then *really* famesque when he cheated on her with the nanny—to the point that *she* was the one who made Balthazar Getty famesque (even though he's the one with the hit TV series, *Brothers & Sisters*) when he reportedly ran off from his wife with her for a while.

But Miller's groundbreaking famesque is threatened. She stars in *G.I. Joe: The Rise of Cobra*, a big dumb movie that opened Friday on 4,007 screens. By now it's possible that 10 million Americans just saw Sienna Miller on the big screen.

What happens then? Will we lose interest? Will she stop saying provocative things? Stop wearing crazy clothes? Stop dating messed-up dudes? (Cohen's not worried: "She has a really great publicist. One of the best in the business.")

Who else is famesque? Set aside that one hit album from a decade ago, and Jessica Simpson pretty much defines it. She's a "singer," but do you know or remember her songs? Likewise her movie roles, most in films that tanked. That cultural-touchstone reality show with husband Nick Lachey? Brief, and canceled four years ago, like their marriage. A 2007 *USA Today*/Gallup poll asked Americans whether they hoped Simpson's "comeback" would succeed; 65 percent said they didn't care one way or the other. But there she is on the cover of *Vanity Fair*, no less, standard-bearer for all those blond stars (Kate Bosworth, Denise Richards) whose love lives are their true art form.

Or "NFL star" Matt Leinart, who, like Anna Kournikova, has done better on the "hottest singles" and "most beautiful" lists than the playing fields. He went to USC, which put him in partying proximity of Paris Hilton. He may never be the starting quarterback again, but he still draws the paparazzi.

The famesque are young, beautiful, and noticeably white—a formula that seems to disproportionately draw the paparazzi and dominate the gossip magazines. One could make the case that the sort-of famesque African American starlet Kerry Washington (so gorgeous! So ubiquitous! What was she in again?) should be more famesque than she is.

One last example—someone who may yet top Sienna Miller in the art of famesque.

Ashton Kutcher.

"But Ashton Kutcher is famous!" you say. "He's a big star!"

Star of *what*? Of the TV commercials, where he plays himself? Of the red carpets, where he clowns and mugs with his beautiful older wife? Of a million great interviews, where with expert calibrations of wit and self-deprecation he divulges how crazy and blessed his life is?

Name one of his movies. Just one. And no, not *Dude, Where's My Car?*, another one.

See? Famesque.

"Increasingly, reality TV shows are no longer just voyeuristic journeys into the failings of real people, but launching pads for fame-seekers looking to parlay publicity—good or bad—into a career."

Reality Television Offers Chances for Fame and Success

Associated Press

In the following viewpoint, the Associated Press asserts that some participants in reality television shows parlay their fifteen minutes of fame into success and profit. The Associated Press suggests that real people who have appeared on Survivor, The Apprentice, *and other programs make a good living for appearances in nightclubs, at conventions, and on television. It continues that contestants who did not win the grand prize, such as Elisabeth Hasselbeck and Bethenny Frankel, have gone on to arguably greater career advancement. The Associated Press is the largest and oldest news organization in the world.*

As you read, consider the following questions:

1. As stated in the viewpoint, what was Jon Dalton's goal in *Survivor*?

Associated Press, "People Seek Fame, Fortune on Reality TV," msnbc.com, September 4, 2008. Reprinted with permission of the Associated Press.

2. What has Omarosa Manigault-Stallworth gained from playing the villain on *The Apprentice*, as described in the viewpoint?

3. How did Sunset Tan benefit from one season as a cable reality show, according to the Associated Press?

When Jon Dalton was discovered by a *Survivor* casting agent at an L.A. gas station several years ago, the chance to win a million dollars wasn't the prize he most desired.

Instead, he relished the chance to showcase "Jonny Fairplay," an immoral jerk persona he developed during his time as a manager in professional wrestling.

"Fairplay" became a hated household name among reality TV audiences, mainly because he lied on air that his grandmother had just died to earn other competitors' sympathies. Catcalling audiences at a reality TV awards show in October seemed to cheer when Danny Bonaduce dropped Dalton on his face onstage, breaking several teeth.

Dalton has sued Bonaduce for battery. But Dalton says, despite the sometimes painful side effects of celebrity, being roundly despised has helped earn him a six-figure annual income.

Dalton said he regularly receives $2,000 to $15,000 to appear at nightclubs, conventions and on other TV shows, partly to satisfy curiosity about whether he's really a jerk in person. It's an income that affords him a three-bedroom house in his hometown of Danville, Va., and the ability to care for his wife and baby daughter.

"I feel personally that I raped reality television and I'm happy about that," Dalton, 34, said in an interview by phone from Danville.

"The million dollars was never my primary goal," Dalton said. "My goal was to create the character of 'Jonny Fairplay' and keep that character on television for as long as possible."

Fame Launching Pads

Increasingly, reality TV shows are no longer just voyeuristic journeys into the failings of real people, but launching pads for fame-seekers looking to parlay publicity—good or bad—into a career.

At a recent open casting call in Costa Mesa, Calif., a shot at fame drove a throng of wannabes to brave the hot sun for the chance to audition for *Survivor*, season 18.

"I want to walk down the street or in the mall and have someone come after me and ask for my autograph," said Shane Cardenes, a 37-year-old high school softball coach from Lake Elsinore, Calif. "I want the paparazzi to come after me."

Several in the crowd rattled off the most famous reality participants to go on to become, well, real stars. Rob and Amber Mariano, who married after being on *Survivor: All-Stars* together, are probably the most well-known reality couple. Rob Mariano is to host a new reality show, *Tontine* this fall, while Amber has appeared in TV commercials and been on the cover of several magazines.

Elisabeth Hasselbeck, another oft-named breakout, turned a 2001 *Survivor* appearance into her co-hosting job on the daytime talk show *The View*.

An appearance on a reality TV show "has the ability to open several doors," said Amber Horn, a 30-year-old Las Vegas bartender who stripped down to her underwear for a video testimonial at the casting call. "You've just got to be crazy enough to kick them open."

Extending Their 15 Minutes

Prolonging the spotlight from a reality show appearance has become a full-time job for booking agent Marc Marcuse of Reel Management. He has represented nearly 300 former reality participants, booking them on other shows, at events and on red carpets.

"When somebody gets off of their show, they always want to capitalize on their fame while they can," Marcuse said.

Regular Joes who get a taste of the fawning attention of camera crews usually don't want to return to their boring former life, said *Survivor* casting director Lynne Spillman. They also get a taste of the money that pure fame can bring.

"More and more people are applying because they want to be on TV," Spillman said.

It's rare for participants not to try to extend their 15 minutes of fame, she said. "They see it as easy money."

After just a few episodes of the first season of *The Apprentice*, participant Omarosa Manigault-Stallworth became a reviled figure. Her in-your-face confrontations included accusing another participant of racism for using the phrase "pot calling the kettle black."

The nonstop catfights lifted the show's ratings and lit up online message boards. Omarosa, who now goes by just her first name, quickly hired a publicist and agent to help her monetize her newfound infamy. She has since been on more than 109 TV episodes—more than many working actors—and she is a regular at celebrity functions around Hollywood.

"People love villains. I'm the naughty girl of reality TV," she said. "They tune in to see me body slam my opponents just like any wrestler."

Appropriately, she is writing a book called *The Bitch Switch*, which is coming out in October. Omarosa said she has shot two more guest appearances for reality shows that will air in the fall, and lectures 15–20 times a year for various groups for an average $10,000 per appearance.

Great for Business

Others have treated the reality format as a dramatized infomercial for publicizing their business.

Sunset Tan on the E! network is a case in point. After just one season on air, the actual tanning salon, whose ditzy sales girls Holly and Molly get flirty with Hollywood actor clients, has sold more than 100 franchises nationwide at $40,000 a pop, said co-owner Devin Haman.

The underlying business has become so profitable, E! became a partner in the franchise profits while the show is on air, Haman said.

"It's a multimillion-dollar commercial," Haman said of the show. "It's amazing to have that."

The cameras have also done little to hurt the healthy baked goods business of Bethenny Frankel. She finished a close second to becoming a Martha Stewart employee on *The Apprentice: Martha Stewart*. But she has since had plenty of exposure for her own cooking business on *The Real Housewives of New York City*, despite being single.

Hits to her Web site have jumped 10 times since her first TV appearance. She's also writing a book, *Naturally Thin*, to come out next year. A tequila maker is in talks to turn her "Skinny Girl Margarita" recipe into an off-the-shelf drink, she said.

"I'm the real winner," Frankel said of coming second in *Martha Stewart*. "I'm so glad I didn't get that job."

❚ *"Reality television exploits situations."*

Reality Television May Not Necessarily Offer Fame and Success

Christopher J. Falvey

Christopher J. Falvey is the author of the VN/VO, a political, social, and media commentary blog. In the following viewpoint, he argues that reality television may have negative impacts on society. He declares that it does not make average people famous— reality television makes situations famous and pegs individuals into preconceived archetypes. Therefore, Falvey dismisses the notion that such shows place authentic or lasting fame within anyone's reach. Reality television endangers cultural norms instead, the author contends, by placing value on inappropriate behaviors and unrealistic circumstances.

As you read, consider the following questions:

1. How does the author define fame?

2. What are "fame archetypes," according to Falvey?

3. In Falvey's view, why are participants in reality television rarely famous?

Christopher J. Falvey, "The Paradox of Reality Television Fame," BC: Blogcritics, May 26, 2005. Reproduced by permission.

"After the break, how to get on a reality television show! Learn the ins and outs of . . ."

I turned off the news program right there. I understand why this would interest a subset of people—they want to be famous. Reality television, supposedly, holds that golden promise that our culture has yearned for eternally: a system where any common person can become famous for doing nothing extraordinary. (Previously, the only way to achieve this brand of fame was to jump wildly behind a television reporter as he or she was reporting from the street.)

The promise, however, is flawed.

"Fame" may be the single most enigmatic entity in modern culture. It may very well be the *most important* entity—a scale in which we judge the worth of most everything. At the same time, it is an entity that is completely impossible to define or predict—from a cause-and-effect standpoint—by any mathematical means. (Note: I use the vague term "entity" not only as a device to spice up this article and make myself seem smart, but really because it would be inaccurate to approach it as anything more specific—its both a living, physical mechanism and a description of a condition.)

Think of it this way. We are a culture obsessed with rankings and statistics. We know the past worth of sports players based on simple mathematics, as well we can predict their future worth with only slightly more complex mathematics. Same, really, for accountants, grocery store clerks, and everything in between. We certainly debate the subtleties of the calculations and mathematical processes used, but we all generally agree that there *exists* some formula for defining worth and value of pretty much anything. Anything except *fame*, that is.

Okay, an important caveat: there has always been a camp of observers and critics who obsess over the coloration between an individual's fame and their talent—the presumption being that the two should somehow match. We argue that certain individuals "really should not be famous" because they have little talent. Or the other side retorts that indeed all famous people are talented, it's just not a talent respected by critics, and that the market defines talent, thus fame and talent are truly synchronized.

The Talent/Fame Paradox

This whole angle of attempting to compare talent and fame, however, misses the real point. The two have nothing to do with each other. Talent is measurable, fame is not. This is because it's not the single individual that is actually "famous." Rather, our culture has *fame archetypes*, which single individuals merely fill. For example, who is Madonna? She's an Italian-American girl from Detroit who happens to enjoy singing and dancing. Everything about her famed persona, however, has nothing to do with her. If Madonna Louise Veronica Ciccone had never been born, "Madonna," as a concept, would still exist. Arguably, whatever "Madonna" is to popular culture has existed well before this individual was born and will exist well after she has faded away—merely filled by different individuals.

Thus, fame really is just an attempt to commodify all of the archetypes we encounter in people. This is all well and good in a conceptual sense—psychologically, humans have always categorized things using sample models. Sparing you, the reader, of a lengthy Advanced Psychology of Human Interaction dissertation (which I'd be making up anyway)—let's put it simply: one cannot possibly know the ins and outs of every person they encounter. They need archetypes, and fame is an offshoot of this need.

Idealism and Exclusion

The increasing popularity and scope of television over the past fifty-plus years has created an interesting predicament. Television, you see, is really a completely different animal than

Reality Stars as Commodities

Watching *American Idol* is like sitting through an endless, commercialized hall of mirrors—it's a real-life version of the over-the-top product placement in *Josie and the Pussycats*. Fox has reaped millions by making *Idol* wannabes literally do backflips over corporate logos, gulp Coke, shampoo with Herbal Essences, and drive Ford Focuses in mini-commercials disguised as music videos. The contestants who succeed are as much commodities as the products they hawk: [Kelly] Clarkson's humble, aw-shucks personality helped her win the *Idol* title, but by the time she promoted her single "Miss Independent" during the show's second season, the producers attempted to remake her hair, makeup, and persona in Christina Aguilera's sexed-up image.

Jennifer L. Pozner
"Reality TV Lets Marketers Write the Script,"
Bitch, no. 24, Spring 2004.

any other medium through which fame—and its individual archetypes of people—can be channeled. Television allows us to access these archetypes using the two senses which we use predominantly to experience, categorize, and judge others: visual and auditory. As well, television was able to package these things in quick and easy-to-digest pieces, while evolving in a nearly infinitely expansive arena. Unlike movies, plays, music, and every other media—television can be *everything*.

Thus, the predicament that television (or, really, the way society insists on television content being structured) creates is that it both becomes the center of our archetypes for all people and it injects idealism and exclusion into the same mix. We don't archetype certain "types" of people; certain flaws don't make good television—or, more generally, don't make good "fame."

Reality Television's Real Revolution

Reality television supposedly "changes everything." Or, so I've been told in all of the special features sections of the variety of reality television DVDs I own. Most of the talk of this supposed revolution in reality television essentially revolves around the breaking down of this very fame archetype I'm discussing. Where fame used to be reserved for idealized personae, it's quickly moving down to the proverbial "normal people"—for better or worse.

All of this may be somewhat true, but I believe this is a flawed premise in terms of the real transformation that has been brought about. Reality television has very little to do with individual personae. Reality television exploits *situations*. So, while it may be somewhat interesting how individuals are positioned in this new format, it is now far less relevant in terms of how viewers intermingle the structure of television with the structure of their own lives—which still occurs at the same accelerated degree as always.

It's as if we've run out of new archetypes of people to fashion within famed individuals. We have a model for everything we care about in that arena, and thus are now fixated—in the same fashion—on situations. Furthermore, like the famed individuals previously the center of popular culture, these situations are quickly being bastardized by idealization and exclusion.

Reality, Edited

Anyone who has even a cursory knowledge of how business is run knows that the situations in *The Apprentice*, while founded somewhat in reality, are at best laughably irrelevant and at worst precariously erroneous. The same goes for, say, the therapeutic processes used in *Starting Over*. While there are certainly many subtle ways a therapist goes about helping abused and psychologically damaged women, something tells me exhibiting said problems on national television is not generally taught in medical school.

Interestingly enough, the individuals in these shows *are* often acting a lot more pragmatically than their fictional "fame archetype" counterparts. This is a lot of the reason why, excepting for a very rare few examples, these individuals are rarely *famous*—using the definition of being inserted into a pre-existing, idealized archetype—for very long. One could actually argue, never at all. The circumstance, however, is famous.

Will this more realistic model of people benefit society? Maybe. What becomes dangerous, though, is that the trade-off remains a completely unrealistic image of situations. Will future businesspeople assume that foolishly inappropriate characteristics—such as the ability to best chew out and expose the flaws [of] your presumed adversary—prove the worth of associates? Will those with psychological problems assume that the only way to heal is to expose said problems nearly to the point of becoming nothing more than a poster child for that problem? Will it be possible to find true love without being locked in an opulent apartment together, attempting to complete foolishly embarrassing tasks?

The issue becomes even more perilous in reverse. Will we, as a culture, place less value on situations that would not make great television? Maybe this seems extreme, but it is already common in general interactions amongst people to use much of the time discussing situations on reality television as if we interacted with these situations ourselves. What, then, is being edited out? Most likely, and ironically enough, *reality*.

Periodical Bibliography

The following articles have been selected to supplement the diverse views presented in this chapter.

Jacob Bernstein   "The Celebrity Cover Backlash," *Daily Beast*, May 18, 2010.

Patrick Brown   "Nobody Wants to Go Home: A Unified Theory of Reality TV," *Millions*, January 26, 2010. www.themillions.com.

Rachel Dodes   "Recession Dims Stars' Style Power," *Wall Street Journal*, September 15, 2009.

Chris Hedges   "The Man in the Mirror," Truthdig.com, July 13, 2009.

Sarah Hepola   "The Year Celebrity Scandal Died," *Salon*, December 26, 2008. www.salon.com.

Michael Hirschorn   "The Case for Reality TV," *Atlantic*, May 2007.

Jemima Kiss   "@ Future of Journalism: What Do We Do with Celebrity News?" *Guardian* (United Kingdom), June 18, 2008.

Hiram Lee   "The 'Balloon Boy' Hoax, Celebrity Culture, and the American Media," World Socialist Web Site, October 22, 2009. www.wsws.com.

Tim Lott   "Tim Lott: The Culture of Celebrity Is Far from Dead—It's Just Growing Up," *Independent* (United Kingdom), January 17, 2010.

Christine Rosen   "The Death of Embarrassment," *In Character*, April 26, 2010. http://incharacter.org.

Allison Hope Weiner   "The Web Site Celebrities Fear," *New York Times*, June 25, 2007.

For Further Discussion

Chapter One

1. Chris Hedges argues that celebrity culture harms Americans by providing unrealistic examples of success and wealth. In contrast, Neal Gabler insists that the lives of celebrities are rich with narratives. In your opinion, which author offers the most compelling argument? Cite examples from the viewpoints in your response.

2. Jeanna Bryner alleges that celebrity culture is on the rise because young people are more narcissistic than previous generations. Do you agree or disagree with Bryner? Explain your answer.

Chapter Two

1. Emily Stimpson contends that youths look to celebrities as proof that success and recognition can be achieved without work. Do you agree or disagree with the author? Explain your response.

2. PR Newswire cites a survey claiming that youths look to parents, coaches, and teachers as role models. In your opinion, is this persuasive evidence to suggest that youths look for heroes that are within their reach? Use examples from the viewpoint to support your answer.

Chapter 3

1. Heribert Dieter and Rajiv Kumar suggest that celebrities' humanitarian efforts and campaigns are too simplistic to impact global problems. In your view, does this include the efforts that Kate Bowman Johnston supports in her viewpoint? Cite examples from the texts to form your response.

2. Emily Sweeney argues that many celebrities participate in philanthropy outside the spotlight, often contributing to their hometowns and other charitable organizations. Gloria Goodale maintains that celebrities do charity work to stay in the spotlight and maintain their status. With which viewpoint do you agree? Explain your response.

Chapter Four

1. Do you agree or disagree with Joseph Epstein that the extreme successes and failures of celebrities help place ordinary life into context? Explain your answer.

2. Amy Argetsinger contends that reputations and personal lives overshadow many celebrities' talents and achievements. In your view, how does this reflect the value of fame today? Cite examples from the viewpoint to illustrate your answer.

3. Christopher J. Falvey asserts that reality television programs are filled with casts and contestants that fit cultural stereotypes. Did the reality television stars described in the Associated Press viewpoint play stereotypical roles? Use examples from the texts to form your response.

Organizations to Contact

The editors have compiled the following list of organizations concerned with the issues debated in this book. The descriptions are derived from materials provided by the organizations. All have publications or information available for interested readers. The list was compiled on the date of publication of the present volume; the information provided here may change. Be aware that many organizations take several weeks or longer to respond to inquiries, so allow as much time as possible.

American Psychological Association (APA)
750 First Street NE, Washington, DC 20002-4242
(800) 374-2721
Web site: www.apa.org

Based in Washington, D.C., the American Psychological Association (APA) is a scientific and professional organization that represents psychology in the United States. With 150,000 members, the APA is the largest association of psychologists worldwide. It publishes articles and reports related to popular culture, celebrities, success, and similar topics in its numerous journals.

Live Earth
8750 Wilshire Boulevard, Ste. 250, Beverly Hills, CA 90211
(310) 550-3888
Web site: http://liveearth.org

Helmed by music producer Kevin Wall and former U.S. vice president and environmental activist Al Gore, the mission of Live Earth is to change consumer behaviors and motivate corporations and political leaders to enact decisive measures to combat the climate crisis. Live Earth promoted a concert series held in July 2007, which was held in different parts of the world and included more than 150 bands and artists.

Not On Our Watch
email: info@notonourwatchproject.org
Web site: www.notonourwatchproject.org

Not On Our Watch is a nonprofit agency that aims to focus global attention and resources toward putting an end to mass atrocities around the world. Drawing on the powerful voices of artists, activists and cultural leaders—including George Clooney, Brad Pitt, Don Cheadle, Matt Damon, Jerry Weintraub, and David Pressman—Not On Our Watch generates lifesaving humanitarian assistance and protection for the vulnerable, marginalized, and displaced.

ONE
1400 Eye Street, Suite 600, Washington, DC   20005
(202) 495-2700
Web site: www.one.org

Supported by Brad Pitt, George Clooney, and Bono, ONE is a coalition made up of more than 2.4 million members and more than one hundred nonprofit, advocacy, and humanitarian organizations. ONE was organized in 2008 when two advocacy groups—Debt, AIDS, Trade Africa (DATA) and the One Campaign—joined forces. ONE's objective is to raise public awareness of global poverty, hunger, disease, and efforts to fight such problems in the world's poorest countries.

People for the Ethical Treatment of Animals (PETA)
501 Front Street, Norfolk, VA   23510
(757) 622-PETA (7382) • fax: (757) 622-0457
Web site: www.peta.org

People for the Ethical Treatment of Animals (PETA), with more than 2 million members and supporters, is the largest animal rights organization in the world. PETA focuses its attention on the four areas in which the largest numbers of animals suffer the most intensely for the longest periods of time: on factory farms, in laboratories, in the clothing trade, and in the entertainment industry. The organization works through public education, cruelty investigations, research, animal rescue, legislation, special events, celebrity involvement, and protest campaigns.

Pop Culture Association/American Culture Association (PCA/ACA)

c/o John F. Bratzel, 276 Bessey Hall, East Lansing, MI   48824
(517) 355-6660 • fax: (517) 355-5250
Web site: http://pcaaca.org

Pop Culture Association/American Culture Association (PCA/ACA) was founded as an offshoot of the American studies movement in the late 1960s. Supporting the study of popular and American culture is an important mission for the organization; therefore, PCA/ACA established an endowment fund to ensure that goal. Drawing from the interest it receives, the PCA/ACA Endowment has been able to support graduate students, international scholars, and research interested in American and popular culture studies.

Raising Malawi

1100 South Robertson Boulevard, Los Angeles, CA   90035
(310) 867-2881
Web site: www.raisingmalawi.org

Raising Malawi is a nongovernmental organization that provides humanitarian aid to the 1 million Malawian orphans living in extreme poverty. Cofounded by Madonna and Kabbalah Centre codirector Michael Berg in 2006, Raising Malawi uses a community-based approach to provide immediate direct physical assistance, create long-term sustainability, support education and psychosocial programs, and build public awareness through multimedia and worldwide volunteer efforts.

Rutherford Institute

PO Box 7482, Charlottesville, VA   22906-7482
(434) 978-3888 • fax: (434) 978-1789

e-mail: staff@rutherford.org
Web site: www.rutherford.org

Founded in 1982 by constitutional attorney and author John W. Whitehead, the Rutherford Institute has emerged as one of the nation's leading advocates of civil liberties and human rights, litigating in the courts and educating the public on a wide spectrum of issues affecting individual freedom in the United States and around the world. It critiques celebrity culture in its articles, which include "John Lennon: A Sacrifice to the Cult of Celebrity," "Michael Jackson, Media Greed and the Demise of Democracy," and "Why the Obsession with Paris Hilton?"

Screen Actors Guild (SAG)
Hollywood—National Headquarters
5757 Wilshire Boulevard, 7th Floor
Los Angeles, CA   90036-3600
(323) 954-1600
Web site: www.sag.org

Established in 1933, the Screen Actors Guild (SAG) exists to enhance actors' working conditions and compensation and benefits, and to advocate artists' rights. With twenty branches nationwide, SAG represents nearly 120,000 actors who work in motion pictures, television, commercials, the video game industry, the Internet, and other media formats.

Bibliography of Books

Robert Clarke, ed. *Celebrity Colonialism: Fame, Power and Representation in Colonial and Postcolonial Cultures.* Newcastle upon Tyne, UK: Cambridge Scholars Publishing, 2009.

Andrew F. Cooper *Celebrity Diplomacy.* Boulder, CO: Paradigm Publishers, 2008.

Susan J. Drucker and Gary Gumpert, eds. *Heroes in a Global World.* Cresskill, NJ: Hampton Press, 2008.

Michael Essany *Reality Check: The Business and Art of Producing Reality TV.* Boston, MA: Focal Press/Elsevier, 2008.

Mitchell Fink *The Last Days of Dead Celebrities.* New York: Miramax Books, 2006.

Jake Halpern *Fame Junkies: The Hidden Truths Behind America's Favorite Addiction.* Boston, MA: Houghton Mifflin Company, 2007.

Daniel Herwitz *The Star as Icon: Celebrity in the Age of Mass Consumption.* New York: Columbia University Press, 2008.

Marina Hyde *Celebrity: How Entertainers Took over the World and Why We Need an Exit Strategy.* London: Harvill Secker, 2009.

Fred Inglis — *A Short History of Celebrity.* Princeton, NJ: Princeton University Press, 2010.

Nathan Dwayne Jackson — *Bono's Politics: The Future of Celebrity Political Activism.* Saarbrücken, Germany: VDM Verlag, 2008.

Matthew Jacob and Mark Jacob — *What the Great Ate: A Curious History of Food and Fame.* New York: Three Rivers Press, 2010.

Marlise Elizabeth Kast — *Tabloid Prodigy.* Philadelphia, PA: Running Press, 2007.

Cooper Lawrence — *The Cult of Celebrity: What Our Fascination with the Stars Reveals About Us.* Guilford, CT: Skirt, 2009.

Susan Murray and Laurie Ouellette, eds. — *Reality TV: Remaking Television Culture.* New York: New York University Press, 2009.

Laurie Ouellette and James Hay — *Better Living Through Reality TV: Television and Post-Welfare Citizenship.* Malden, MA: Blackwell Pub., 2008.

Tom Payne — *Fame: What the Classics Tell Us About Our Cult of Celebrity.* New York: Picador, 2010.

Kathryn Petras and Ross Petras — *Unusually Stupid Celebrities: A Compendium of All-Star Stupidity.* New York: Villard, 2007.

Drew Pinsky and S. Mark Young — *The Mirror Effect: How Celebrity Narcissism Is Seducing America.* New York: HarperCollins, 2009.

Sean Redmond and Su Holmes, eds.	*Stardom and Celebrity: A Reader.* Thousand Oaks, CA: Sage Publications, 2007.
Jim Rubens	*OverSuccess: Healing the American Obsession with Wealth, Fame, Power, and Perfection.* Austin, TX: Greenleaf Book Group Press, 2009.
David Shields	*Reality Hunger: A Manifesto.* New York: Alfred A. Knopf, 2010.
Gary Stromberg and Jane Merrill	*The Harder They Fall: Celebrities Tell Their Real-Life Stories of Addiction and Recovery.* Center City, MN: Hazelden, 2008.

Index